Planning and Conducting Agency-Based Research

A Workbook for Social Work Students in Field Placements

Second Edition

Alex Westerfelt
University of Kansas

Tracy J. Dietz
Texas Christian University

Allyn and Bacon
Boston London Toronto Sydney Tokyo Singapore

About the Authors

Alex Westerfelt is assistant professor at the School of Social Welfare, University of Kansas, where he teaches undergraduate and graduate research courses.

Tracy J. Dietz is associate professor of social work and director of field education at Texas Christian University, where she teaches undergraduate research, field seminar, and practice courses.

Copyright © 2001 by Allyn & Bacon
A Pearson Education Company
160 Gould Street
Needham Heights, Massachusetts 02494-2130

Internet: www.abacon.com

ISBN 0-8013-3415-2

Printed in the United States of America

10 9 8 7 6 5 4 3 2   03 02 01 00

CONTENTS

Section XIII: Writing the Final Paper   173

Bibliography   181

INTRODUCTION

Social work educators are aware that graduates of social work programs rarely *use* research findings in their practice and even less often *conduct* research in their practice (Epstein, 1987; Kirk, 1990; Kirk & Fisher, 1976). In a survey of field instructors regarding assessment of their MSW students' skills in social work practice, the field instructors rated understanding of research as the lowest skill area for students (Knight, 1993). In a survey of potential employers' views of the ideal undergraduate curriculum, agency personnel rated research as their least valued content area (Forte & Mathews, 1994). Furthermore, the National Institute of Mental Health (NIMH) Task Force on Social Work Research asserts that there is a crisis in social work research, claiming that at all levels of social work education, the teaching of research skills is inadequate (Report of the NIMH Task Force on Social Work Research, 1991).

Yet the contexts in which social work practice occurs increasingly demand that social workers be proficient in evaluating intervention outcomes. Although course work in research methods is an essential component of social work education, students should also have opportunities to apply research knowledge and skills outside the classroom, ideally in their field placement (Strom & Gingerich, 1993). As Fraser, Lewis, and Norman (1990) note: "For many schools, the development of a sophisticated research curriculum with opportunities to apply research skills in a supervised practice setting remains an unfulfilled challenge" (p. 100).

We developed this workbook in response to that challenge. Its purpose is to provide undergraduate and graduate social work faculty and students a systematic series of research assignments leading to a completed research study that students could carry out in their field placements. These assignments have three ultimate goals: (1) to increase students' interest and skills in practice research; (2) to help students produce agency-based research that contributes to the mission of the agency; and (3) to demonstrate to students the value and utility of practice-based research. Our premise is that once students experience success in carrying out a research project in a practice setting and see the usefulness of their findings, they will have the confidence and motivation to continue research efforts in their own postgraduate practice.

Social work has long recognized the importance of field education as a means for integrating knowledge and practice skills. We believe that the field setting also provides students an ideal opportunity to apply research concepts and methods learned in research courses and to see firsthand how their research projects can benefit clients and agencies. For a practitioner, conducting research in the field can lead to an understanding of the real importance that research results can have in daily practice.

Agency-Based Research

This workbook is designed to aid students in planning and conducting research projects based in an agency setting. We define agency-based research as applied research with the goal of producing information that can be used to improve conditions and services for clients. This is in contrast to basic research, which seeks to generate theory or lead to a deeper understanding of an issue (i.e., knowledge for the sake of knowledge). Agency-based research involves studying some aspect of the agency and its programs or its clients and their communities with an emphasis on the utility of that information. Applied research should inform action, enhance decision making, and lead to solutions of human and societal problems (Patton, 1990).

New in this Edition

In this edition, we include a new section that directly addresses outcomes evaluation (**Section IX**). In addition, this edition features more examples for students to follow, including a list of research questions of projects undertaken by our students, a fully annotated example of a literature review, examples of how to use existing literature, sample consent forms, and a time line for students to plan their project. We have also added resources for locating established research instruments and measures. Based on feedback from our students and others, we believe the second edition of the workbook is even more user-friendly and will be a valuable tool in planning and conducting agency-based research.

Designing an Agency-Based Research Project:
LAYOUT OF THE WORKBOOK

If you want to know . . .

Turn to . . .

✓ What research has the agency
   already done?

✓ What data does the agency
   routinely collect?

Section I:
*Orientation to
Agency Research*

✓ How do I develop a research question?

Section III:
The Research Question

✓ What has already been written
   about this topic?

Section IV:
The Literature Review

✓ What is the best way
   to answer my question?

Section V:
Choosing Your Methodology

See also . . .
→ **Section VI:** *Survey Research*
→ **Section VII:** *Qualitative Research*
→ **Section VIII:** *Single Subject Design*
→ **Section IX:** *Outcomes Evaluation*

✓ How do I choose who to study?

Section X:
Sample Design

✓ What procedures must I put in place
   to safeguard research participants?

Sections II & XI:
Protection of Research Participants

✓ How do I analyze my findings?

Section XII:
Data Analysis

✓ How do I present my
   results and conclusions?

Section XIII:
Writing the Final Paper

We would like to thank the following people for their suggestions for the second edition of the workbook: Ineke Way, University of Michigan; Arlene Kaplan Brown, Florida International University; Patricia Kolar, University of Pittsburgh; and C.G. Kledaras, Campbell University. We also thank our editor at Allyn & Bacon, Judith S. Fifer. We received helpful comments on earlier versions of the workbook from: Tara V. Bankston, Louisiana State University; Cynthia Leonard Bishop, Meredith College; William Cloud, University of Denver; Nancie Palmer, Washburn University; Gregory Pettys, Washburn University; Steven Rose, Louisiana State University; James Stafford, University of Mississippi; and Barbara Key Wickell, University of Illinois at Chicago. We appreciate comments from participants who attended our workshop on agency-based research at the 1994 Baccalaureate Program Directors' Meetings in San Francisco and from students who have used earlier drafts and the first edition of the workbook in planning and conducting their agency research projects. Finally, thanks go to Tom Barton for his comments.

HOW TO USE THIS WORKBOOK

To use this workbook effectively, students should either have completed a research methods course or currently be enrolled in one. Although the workbook is designed to follow the basic steps of the research process as covered by any research methods text, it is not a research textbook and will not provide all the necessary information to conduct a research project. Rather, it asks the questions students must answer as they plan and conduct a research study. We intend that the workbook be used in conjunction with a research text, and throughout the workbook we remind students to draw upon their text.

The workbook provides guidelines for the development of four methods commonly used in agency-based research including survey research, qualitative research, single-subject design research, and program outcomes evaluation. For each method, we outline the steps we think necessary for completing a research study utilizing that method. We recognize that the steps laid out in this workbook may differ from those presented in other texts, but we expect that the differences will be slight. Further, we recognize that there are many acceptable ways of conducting research.

For each step of the research process we detail what students should cover when writing that section of the research paper. There are two options for the actual writing of the workbook exercises. One option is for students to use the workbook pages to compile their beginning thoughts and ideas. The perforated pages allow them to turn in their work for instructor feedback. Based on instructor feedback, students can then begin their drafts of their research papers. A second option is for students to use the workbook pages to compile their beginning thoughts and ideas and then to use word processing for more thoughtful first drafts. These drafts can use the outline numbering of each workbook section for consistency and structure. The advantages of this option are to provide the instructor with typed copy, and once the instructor provides feedback, to allow students to incorporate it into their draft documents more easily. By the time the students have completed the workbook, they will each have a substantial draft of their final paper.

Because the terms *field instructor*, *field supervisor*, and *field liaison* are often used interchangeably, we want to clarify the terms we use. In the workbook, *field instructor* is used to refer to the agency staff member who is responsible for supervising the student. *Course instructor* refers to the university faculty member who is teaching the course in which the workbook is being used. *Field liaisons* are typically university faculty members whose role is to coordinate the students' learning experiences in both the agency and the university. A program may give different responsibilities to different individuals; for example, a program may provide a significant role for a field liaison in the research project. When there are variations from the definitions or names given here, it would be helpful to designate for students the individuals who correspond to the course instructor and the field instructor as identified in the workbook.

Special Note to Students

We have two suggestions for you. First, reiterating what we have stated above, we recommend that from the very beginning you do all the writing for this project on a personal computer using a word processing package. Our students have repeatedly said that this was the single most helpful suggestion we gave them, saving them hours of time in completing the final draft of their paper. If you type a draft of each section and save it on disk, then revise each section after receiving feedback from others, all you should need to do for your final paper is to put the sections together and make minor edits.

Our second suggestion is that while using the workbook to guide your research project, you make a habit of referring to both your research text and the suggested article for the particular method of study you choose. In the Table of Contents you will see the four methods listed. At the beginning of each of the sections we have indicated a specific article that will provide you with an example of a research study that utilizes that method. Reference to your methods text is intended for review of material; reference to the article will give you a complete picture of an actual study and examples of how to write sections of your own study.

Keep in mind that the research process is an ongoing feedback loop. As it is explained, it may appear quite linear, but in actuality, research activities may not follow the orderly steps we present. Inevitably, you will find yourself returning to prior steps to revise them based on what you have found in later steps. Eventually the pieces of the puzzle will all fit together. Trust us. We have designed the workbook in an easy-to-follow, step-by-step format that we believe demystifies the research process. We hope it will build your confidence in your ability to participate in and conduct research in an agency setting.

Special Note to Course Instructors

The workbook can be used in a variety of courses. It is an obvious addition to a research course, but we intentionally designed it for use in a field seminar or a practice course that is taken concurrently with field activity. We encourage faculty to experiment with various options for coverage of this material. The following social work program components are considerations for determining the ideal format: research course requirements and expectations, block versus concurrent placements, the proximity of placements to each other, the primary instructor, and the other people involved in guiding the student project.

Some course instructors, faced with certain program constraints, may want students to complete only a research proposal and not actually carry out the project. Others may want students to work in groups and complete group research projects. In large programs where individual agencies may have several students in placement, students could work together on one project for the agency.

A computer template is available to course instructors who adopt the workbook. The template includes the sections of the workbook assignments and may be used with your students. The purpose of the template is to enable students to more readily move their thoughts and ideas from the pages of the workbook to a computer for word processing. We hope that this aid will encourage students to utilize computers and will help them as they organize and write the first drafts of their papers. Once the first draft is on computer, revisions should be much easier for students. Further, course instructors may find typed drafts of the workbook assignments easier to read and evaluate. If you are interested in obtaining the template, you may contact Tracy Dietz at T.Dietz@tcu.edu.

Special Note to Field Instructors

You are a key player in your students' research projects. Your view of research and the value you place on it will affect their experiences with agency research. However, you will not be totally responsible for helping them conduct the research project. The course instructor is responsible for teaching the students basic research methods and the application of these to agency settings.

Your role is to support and monitor the students along the way. You will be able to provide the best assistance if you are involved from the beginning. The steps we outline in the workbook promote your involvement by requiring students to ask questions of you and other agency staff. Your comments and feedback to them are necessary and will be extremely helpful.

You are an expert about your agency and its clients. You know what questions, if answered, will provide information that will benefit the clients. You may also be an expert in conducting research. However, you do not need a strong research background to work with students. If you lack confidence in your ability to help them with research projects, this workbook will serve as a resource to you as well.

Research resources for field instructors are available from faculty members. You could request that your school present a seminar for field instructors that focuses on conducting agency research. In addition, we provide a bibliography at the end of the workbook for more information on conducting agency-based research.

A Final Note

We would like to hear about your experiences using the workbook. Your comments about what was most helpful and least helpful will help us improve future editions. Please send your comments to us. Include the course for which the workbook was assigned and which sections of the workbook were unclear or difficult to complete. We look forward to hearing from you! Tracy Dietz, TCU Department of Social Work, Texas Christian University, Box 298750, Fort Worth, Texas, 76129, or T.Dietz@tcu.edu.

ORIENTATION
TO AGENCY RESEARCH

Two major arguments support the need for incorporating a research perspective into one's practice. First, our professional code of ethics emphasizes the responsibility of social workers to understand, utilize, and conduct research. Accordingly, professional responsibility requires that we draw on and contribute to the knowledge base of social work.

Second, we are accountable to those we seek to assist. We are responsible for knowing the struggles, needs, and assets of those we assist and for providing the services that make a difference. Only through our continuous search for better understanding and the testing of current understanding can we effectively assist others.

As part of the curriculum in your social work program, you have been exposed to various aspects of research. Much of the information you have acquired is the result of others' research endeavors. In addition, you have either taken a specific research methods class or are currently enrolled in one. Now you are ready to move beyond the role of consumer of research to that of producer of research by conducting a research project at your field placement.

The best way to begin this process is by familiarizing yourself with the research efforts that have already been undertaken at your agency. To that end, we provide the following questions for you to consider as you begin your research project.

Starting with your field instructor (a must!) and proceeding to individuals he or she recommends, ask agency staff about the agency's own research program. You may need to ask more than one person to get a clear picture. Always be sure to indicate to whom you spoke and that person's position title.

If the agency has a research program, complete the questions in Part A. If the agency does not have a research program, complete the questions in Part B.

NAME: DATE:

(A)   If the agency has a research program

(1)   What are its goals and purposes?

(2)   Who is responsible for overseeing agency research? Interview that person, and ask whether the research is done in-house or contracted out. If in-house, what is the size of the research budget? How many staff are involved in research activities?   If done by contract, how often have studies been done in the past and by whom?

(3)   What resistance, if any, from staff and/or clients has been encountered in agency research efforts?

(4)   How does the agency distribute its research findings and to whom? Who has a "right" to see the findings? How does a person obtain a copy of study findings?

(5)   How have staff members used the findings?

(6)   What changes at the agency have resulted from research findings?

(7)   What is the agency process for obtaining permission to conduct a research study? (If there is no agency process in place, we encourage you to obtain written permission to carry out your study from the director of the agency. The procedures for study approval and protecting human subjects are discussed in **Sections II** and **XI**.)

(8)   What studies or reports have been done at the agency? Obtain copies of two recent reports, indicate the purpose of each, and write a one or two sentence summary of each report.

REPORT 1:	REPORT 2:

Now, go to section (C).

(B) If the agency does not have a research program

(1)   Find out if the agency collects and compiles data for annual reports, funding reports, or community public relations. This may involve counts of people who use the agency's services, characteristics of service users, needs assessments, client satisfaction studies, etc. What information has the agency collected? If there have been no data collection efforts, explore why that is.

(2)   How is the collected information used and by whom is it used?

(3)   How does the agency distribute this information and to whom? How have staff used the information?

(4)   What changes at the agency have resulted from the information?

(5) What is the agency process for obtaining permission to conduct a research study? (If there is no agency process in place, we encourage you to obtain written permission to carry out your study from the director of the agency. The procedures for study approval and protecting human subjects are discussed in **Sections II** and **XI**.)

(6) What reports have been done at the agency? Obtain copies of two recent reports, indicate the purpose of each, and write a one or two sentence summary of each report.

REPORT 1:	REPORT 2:

(C) Staff views and usage of research

Interview two staff members, one of whom should be your field instructor.

(1) How do they view research? Write their responses here, indicating their names and position titles.

NAME:	NAME:
TITLE:	TITLE:

(2)   How do they use research to improve practice?

(3) What research-oriented journals or books are frequently used by them? How often do they read these journals?

(4) Ask each person about a specific article he or she has used in the past month and how the information was used.

(D) Agency resources for your research

What are the agency resources that will be available to you as you conduct your research project? Indicate below what you find out about staff assistance (clerical, computer, etc.), photocopying, mail, computer access, and anything else that may be relevant.

PROTECTION OF RESEARCH PARTICIPANTS (PRELIMINARY)

We have included two sections on the protection of research participants. We want you to consider safeguards for participants from the initial conception of your study through its completion. We find that students (and even seasoned researchers) are in a better position to prepare applications for review of participant safeguards and study procedures once they have designed their study. However, time constraints may require you to submit materials **before** the study is completely designed. Consequently, we introduce the process early on so that you can explore university and agency requirements. Then, in **Section XI** we guide you through the basic requirements for protection of research participants.

Protection of the people who participate in a research study is a primary responsibility of the researcher. This obligation is generally fulfilled through the use of a consent form and through the early peer review of the researcher's study, via submission of the proposed study to a review committee. These review committees are typically called Institutional Review Boards (IRBs), but some universities may have another name for their review committee. Agencies may or may not have research review committees as well. The responsibility of the IRB is to review all research involving "human subjects." (We prefer the term ***research participants*** which keeps with our emphasis on the participation and contribution of clients in the research process.) You cannot proceed with data collection until you have approval from the IRB.

Federal regulations provide the basis for IRB procedures and the actual evaluation of study safeguards, but the regulations leave room for varying interpretation. Thus, our discussion is necessarily general rather than specific, and the exercises that follow will direct you in learning more about your specific IRB.

You must submit your study design for review **before** you begin collecting data. Some IRBs have strict time frames for review of and response to submissions. As

---

NAME: DATE:

noted above, this may necessitate a submission from you **before** you have had time to complete the necessary sections of this workbook and develop your study design. In that case, you need to work closely with your course instructor to meet the IRB requirements.

Keep in mind that it is **not** the function of these committees to evaluate your study design and methods, but rather to evaluate the extent to which you will protect research participants from any harm. This includes physical, social, psychological, and legal harm.

For example, if you are studying people recently paroled from prison, how will you make sure they do not feel any coercion to participate in your study? What if they mistakenly believe that their parole officer **expects** them to participate? For some studies you must address how you will handle information you receive that involves illegal behaviors. You will always have to discuss how you will keep information confidential.

Consider what is needed if your study involves sensitive information. For example, if you ask information about past sexual assault and a person becomes emotionally upset, what are your plans to handle that type of situation? As part of your application for IRB approval, you must describe all potential risks involved in your study and the procedures for protecting against or minimizing those risks, including risks to confidentiality.

REMINDER:
Build enough time into your study's time table to allow the IRB to review your application.

(A) The university IRB

Find out the name of the university IRB and contact its chairperson regarding application for approval of your study's procedures. Obtain a copy of the application packet to review and begin preparing. Be sure to ask about the time frames for submission of applications and the expected date for response.

Indicate below with whom you talked and what information you received.

(B) The agency IRB

Find out the agency's procedure for the review and approval of research studies. Ask for a copy of the procedures for submission. Also ask about the time frames for submission of applications and the expected date for response.

If the agency has no formalized procedures, we strongly encourage you to submit the University IRB application to the agency, and obtain, in writing, the agency director's permission to carry out your study.

Indicate the names of those with whom you talked and what information you received.

(C) Prepare a time line for your human subjects' review application

If you need to submit your application for approval of study procedures very soon, consult the IRB guidelines and turn to **Section XI** to prepare your application.

DATE

First draft of IRB application to your course instructor
Receive comments from your course instructor and make corrections based on instructor feedback.

* First IRB application to University IRB committee

Agency application due

* First IRB notification on your application expected
Once application is approved, data collection can begin. Keep in mind that you may have to make revisions and resubmit.

If applicable, resubmission due

If applicable, final IRB approval expected

REMINDER:
   * *After course instructor approval, add the starred dates to your study time line on page 68.*

THE RESEARCH QUESTION

In this section you will develop your initial research question. We say "initial" because oftentimes as people begin looking at articles related to their topic of interest, they learn more about the topic or about ways it has been studied that help them reshape their research question. We want to help you to brainstorm possible questions of interest to you.

Keep in mind that a research question is not the same as a hypothesis. A hypothesis is your expectation about how events or phenomena will be related, ***based on some prior study and understanding of the events or phenomena.*** A research question is just that, a question. It asks exactly what you would like to know, ***not*** what is already known or what can be expected. A hypothesis is a statement. A research question is a question.

Social workers assess client strengths and successes as readily as they assess problems and needs. As you think about possible questions for your study, consider research questions that seek to learn not only about problems and needs, but also about strengths and successes. We encourage this approach in research.

Discovering how people survive stressful situations and crises contributes valuable information to the profession as it develops programs and services. Uncovering the strengths of certain types of families or communities can enhance workers' practice knowledge. Allowing people to tell their stories in their own words not only recognizes that they have much to offer but also reminds us that research, like practice, can benefit from a cooperative, interactive approach. We strongly encourage you to be as interested in "what is going right" as in "what is going wrong."

Answering each of the following questions will guide you in developing your research question. As ideas come to mind, put them in question form.

NAME: DATE:

(A) What would you like to know?

(1)   Perhaps you are interested in knowing more about the clients who are served by the agency:

        —their characteristics

        —their strengths and assets

        —their specific needs

        —their satisfaction with the agency's services

        —the obstacles they face, either in daily living
          or in accessing services

        —how clients are affected by agency services
          or lack of agency services

        —other

(2)   Perhaps you are interested in knowing more about the services at
your agency:
   —the extent to which services address the needs
   of people in the community
   —their success in reaching the target population
   —the impact or effectiveness (outcomes) of services
   —other

(3)   Perhaps you are interested in knowing more about the workers at the
agency:
   —their practice orientation
   —their job satisfaction
   —other

(B) What would the agency like to know?

(1) Talk to your field instructor (a must!) or anyone else at the agency she or he recommends as a good source of information for this question. Jot down their ideas for research they think would be of value to the agency. Be open to all their ideas and begin thinking of possible research questions that might blend their interests with yours.

Indicate the names of people to whom you spoke and their position in the agency. What topics are they interested in? Put their ideas into questions.

NAME:	FEEDBACK:

(2) What do they think about your ideas for a research question? Indicate their feedback below.

NAME:	FEEDBACK:

(C) What would the clients like to know?

Check with your field instructor (a must!) about talking to some of the clients with whom you have contact. If you don't yet have contact, ask your field instructor to recommend to you some clients with whom you could talk about this.

Our students' experiences have been that using the word "research" can be as confusing to clients as to students. So, we recommend that you avoid using the word "research" when talking with them. Rather, tell clients that as a student, you are interested in gathering information that would be helpful to the agency. Ask them what topics they think might be helpful for the agency to know more about.

Indicate the first names or initials of people to whom you spoke. What topics would they be interested in learning more about? Put their ideas into questions.

NAME/INITIALS:	FEEDBACK:

(D) What is your research question?

Now take your first stab at coming up with a research question. Based on your thinking, interests, and discussions with others, write out one or two questions you would be interested in pursuing.

Following, we provide some research questions that our students have studied, along with the design type of the study they conducted.

LIST OF STUDENT RESEARCH QUESTIONS
& DESIGN TYPE

How Do Nurse Case Managers and Social Worker Case Managers Describe Case Management Roles? (Qualitative)

What Is the Employee Turnover and Job Satisfaction in the Field of Disabilities? (Survey)

How Does Staff Training Improve Staff Knowledge about Sexuality for People with Disabilities? (Outcomes Evaluation)

What Is Foster Parent Satisfaction of Case Management Services Provided by Private Versus Public Agencies? (Survey)

How Does Attitudinal Change Relate to Length of Stay for Substance Abusers in Treatment? (Survey)

What Is the Effect of Classroom Reinforcement on Classroom Behavior Change? (Single-Subject Design)

What Are the Ethical Restrictions on Dual Relationships among Different Mental Health Professions? (Qualitative)

What Are the Factors Leading to Relapse in Women Who Are Chemically Addicted? (Qualitative)

How Effective Is a Cultural Consciousness-Raising Group on Empowerment of Latino Women? (Outcomes Evaluation)

What Are the Characteristics of Programs in Public Administration Offices for Court Appointed Guardians? (Survey)

What Are the Experiences of Clients with Severe and Persistent Mental Illness Who Are in Community Corrections? (Qualitative)

What Are the Characteristics of Juvenile Offender Recidivists? (Survey)

What Are the Differences and Needs of Peer Leaders Versus Professional Leaders of Self-Help Groups? (Survey)

What Are the Needs of Jewish Elders? (Survey)

(E)   Browse the literature related to your topic

Now make a quick trip to the library just to see what information is available on your topic. This is *not* the time to do a thorough literature review; that will come later. For now, simply see if there are several current articles on your topic and choose two (preferably from social work journals). Don't hesitate to ask reference librarians for help.

Skimming over these articles will give you an idea of the scope of the topic you have chosen and may help you in narrowing down your question. Our experience is that many students significantly change their question based on this first view of the literature. If, in the middle of this step—or the next one—you become less than enthusiastic about your research question, do not hesitate to abandon it and pursue another.

List the author, title, and reference information for two articles you examined and a two- or three-sentence summary of each one.

(1)   Author and Date _____

       Title _____

       Citation Information _____

       _____

       Summary:

(2)   Author and Date _____

       Title _____

       Citation Information _____

       _____

       Summary:

(F) Refine your research question

Refine your Research Question using the following checklist:

☐ Is the research question relevant to social work? How does the issue involve social work?

☐ What makes this issue or problem significant? What is the scope of the issue? (Who is affected? How many people are affected? In what ways?)

☐ By answering your question, how could the information impact services to clients at your agency or improve practice?

☐ Is a study to answer your question feasible? Can you reasonably do what is necessary to answer your research question? You need to consider and address this question relative to the time you have been given to do the study, money that is available for expenses of the study (for example, photocopying, mailing), ethical and logistical considerations, the amount of assistance you will need from others (interviewers, computer consultation, practice consultation), and the amount of cooperation you will need from agency personnel. Be realistic in your estimations because it may help you focus a research question that is too ambitious.

☐ Which research method will you use? Finally, begin to think about the best way (research method) to answer your question. Would qualitative or quantitative methods be most appropriate? (Don't hesitate to return to your methods text for a quick review of these approaches.) This workbook offers guidance on four methods of research: survey, qualitative, single-subject design, and outcomes evaluation. Which method do you think would provide the best information to answer your question? Why?

(G) Write your research question below

Now, share your research question with your peers and field instructor, soliciting their feedback.

Indicate below the names of people you asked for feedback and what questions or suggestions they had.

NAME:	FEEDBACK:

Obtain your course instructor's signature indicating that he/she has approved your research question.

Course Instructor's Sign-off:

THE LITERATURE REVIEW

The purpose of the literature review is to help you become more knowledgeable about your research topic. You will conduct a better study if you know what other people have said about your topic, what they have found in their own studies, and how they designed their studies.

Quantitative methods typically involve a deductive approach to research. Thus, you begin by reviewing the literature to develop your ideas regarding what information to collect in your study. In *qualitative* research, there is a debate about when to review the literature. Some proponents of *qualitative* research suggest doing the literature review later in the study. According to this view, your research will be "pure" in the sense that it will not be guided or biased—perhaps in a wrong direction—by what is known about your topic and what has been done by other researchers. Other *qualitative* researchers value the early review of literature to better understand the topic and to design the best possible study.

We believe that reviewing the literature first is essential, and we guide you in completing that step before you proceed with the other steps of your study whether you are conducting a quantitative or qualitative study. This way you can compare your plans for your study to what others have done with an eye for improving your project. A literature review can keep you from "reinventing the wheel" by suggesting ways to conceptualize (define) the question and operationalize (measure) the variables. The literature will also help you identify existing measurement instruments.

While a considerable part of the literature review is conducted early, remember to think of the literature review as an ongoing process. As your project unfolds and new questions arise, you will return to the literature for answers.

We assume you have access to a college library and computerized databases of abstracts and indexes relevant to social work, and that you are able (or will learn) to use them. Before sitting down at the keyboard, review your research question and remind yourself to stay focused. Electronic searching is powerful and fast, but you can easily overdo it by locating literature that is at best peripheral to your topic. Select only relevant literature.

NAME: DATE:

RESEARCH QUESTION:

Some Considerations:

✓ Students often have difficulty determining whether an article is empirical or not. An empirical article reports the results of an actual study that was designed and completed by the authors. The authors provide information about the people who were in their sample, how the data were collected, and the findings. With few exceptions, the article will contain tables of data or, in the case of qualitative studies, excerpts from participant interviews. We recommend that you locate at least four articles about original research studies that provide as much information as possible about the design and execution of the study. They will provide examples to assist you in designing your study.

Some articles will report findings from other studies. These are *not* empirical articles as they usually do not contain information about how the study was conducted. However, the article will include the source of the empirical articles they are citing.

✓ "I can't find anything on my topic! There have been no studies done on this at all." This is the most common difficulty reported by students doing a literature review. Yes, often students cannot find anything; but it is seldom true that no work has been done on the topic.

What we frequently find is that either the student has not sought the assistance of reference librarians who can help tailor a search of the literature, or the student is too narrowly restricting the search. For example, if the research question is to determine the needs of a community of First Nations people for their local service center, there may be no other published needs assessment of that group. However, you can probably find published studies of the needs of First Nations people in general—for example, surveys regularly conducted by the Indian Health Service. Also you can locate articles that detail needs assessments done among other ethnic groups. Such articles, while not addressing your target group, will provide you with information on how to conduct a needs assessment with an identified group of individuals.

✓ We encourage students to focus their efforts on identifying articles rather than books because articles are easier to digest. The exception concerns edited books that often contain, in essence, a series of articles on the particular topic. Books that are complete reports of a single study or a series of studies can also be helpful. Dissertations completed by persons outside your own university can be very hard to obtain in a timely fashion. (They are sometimes identified in search results simply with the designation, Ph.D. or D.S.W.)

✓ Last, you will find one of the best sources for references at the end of each article. All articles and books will list their references, and once you have identified a relevant work, its bibliography will provide you with several other sources of material. This is why finding the most recent literature is important. Authors are only able to cite works prior to their own.

A word of warning: Too often students have spent many hours, even days, in the library and come to us in frustration because they have nothing to show for their efforts. Do not make the same mistake. Start your search early and regularly seek help. Consult with your librarians and instructors frequently; that's why we are here. Remember: *Seek assistance at the first sign that you are not getting anywhere!*

You should include a minimum of 10 references, no less than four empirical articles (actual studies with sample, methods, and findings), and at least six other scholarly references. The dates of publication of articles should be within the past five years. There are some exceptions to this—for example, a "classic" work that was written many years ago. Also, in a few cases you may find that your topic has rarely been studied and requires a search beyond the past five years.

REMINDER:

Be sure that you know how to conduct a computerized literature search using electronic databases in the library. Do not simply do a search on the Internet. Ask reference librarians for assistance. They can save you much time. Librarians have often told us that they wish students would be less hesitant about asking for help and would seek help earlier, before getting so frustrated. Use your librarians; they are a valuable resource.

(A)   Conduct a literature search

The following directions will guide you step-by-step through the process of locating literature relevant to your research question.

(1)   Ask your course instructor if he/she can recommend any faculty members who are knowledgeable about the topic of your study or population of interest. Talk to suggested faculty members, your field instructor, and other people at your agency to obtain their recommendations for references. Sometimes, locating the right person can give you the bulk of your references.

Indicate with whom you talked, when, and the results.

(2)   Begin searching the literature in the library by choosing key search words.

List them here (ask your professor and/or librarian for their advice):

_____   _____

_____   _____

_____   _____

_____   _____

(3)   List here the databases you will use for your search. Obtain information on how to access them, if you do not know already.

(4) Go to your first database and begin entering the requested information.

    (a) Set the computer search so that it returns the abstract for each reference. This will help you to do the initial gleaning of the list.

    (b) Limit your search to the last five years to start. If that does not generate enough references, do not be too quick to go back more years. Rather, reconsider your search words first.

    (c) If you use the PsychLit abstracts, in the P.T. field, publication type, you can specify empirical study, and it will limit the search to return empirical studies only.

(5) Search!

If the search results include significantly more than about 40 or 50 references, you will need to further narrow your search words so that you have a manageable list of references to review. Do not hesitate to get assistance with this task.

(6) Once you have a successful search list, read through it several times.

    (a) First, read the abstracts in the list and highlight references that appear to be on target with your question.

    (b) Next, highlight any article that is titled "A Review of...." It will provide an overview of the literature related to your topic and can save you much time.

    (c) Go through the list again and examine all the abstracts for sources that seem related to your research question, even if only in part. Mark those that appear to be worth examining.

(7)   Submit the results of your computer search to your instructor for feedback, circling the references you intend to use and starring the empirical articles.

Be sure to write your research question on the top of your computer search list.

(8)   Select and locate the 10 sources you and your instructor have decided will be most relevant. You should start to track down your literature very soon; some sources will have to be obtained from another library, which may require as much as two or three weeks.

(9)   Finally, when you have some literature in hand, among those sources that are most closely related to your research question, choose the most current and examine the authors' references at the end. This will help you identify other relevant sources.

(B)   Critique the literature

Your literature review should be a summary of what each author says—not a series of long, direct quotations—and your evaluation of their work as it relates to your study.

For each source, the following sets of questions will help as you explore the literature. The first set is to use with empirical articles, the second set with nonempirical articles. We have included a blank literature form for you to use with empirical articles and a blank literature form for nonempirical articles. We have also included examples for both types of articles.

We recommend that you photocopy the blank forms for use with additional sources.

(1)   For empirical studies

Author and Date _____

Title _____

Citation Information _____

_____

(a)   What is the purpose of this study and how is it related to your study?

(b)   What theory or theories (if any) does the author use in this study? How might you apply this theory to your topic of study?

(c)   In a brief paragraph describe *how* the sample was obtained.

(d)   Include a brief description of the sample (size, gender, race, age, socioeconomic class, special characteristics), paying close attention to the inclusion and representation of people of color, frequently underrepresented in research. (For example, are people of color included in sufficient numbers, or are several groups simply pooled together with only white and nonwhite comparisons reported?)

(e)   What are the major concepts in the study and the variables chosen to represent each concept?

(f)   Indicate the specific measures used (operationalization) for each of the major variables in the article that are relevant to your study. Begin with the dependent variables if dependent and independent variables are included. If the article is an evaluation of an intervention, briefly describe the intervention (usually the independent variable).

(g)   Describe the method of data collection.

(h)   Summarize the findings of the study in two or three sentences.

(i)   What will you apply from this study to your own? How might you use its strengths or compensate for its limitations?

SAMPLE FOR EMPIRICAL STUDIES

Author and Date Roberts, C.S., Piper, L., Denny, J., & Cuddeback, G. (1997)

Title A Support Group Interv. to Facilitate Young Adults' Adjust. to Cancer

Citation Information Health and Social Work, (22)2, 133-141.

(a)   What is the purpose of this study and how is it related to your study?

Purpose of the study: to evaluate the effectiveness of an intervention for young cancer patients. The goal of the intervention is to reduce psychological stress and improve coping skills and quality of life.

Relates to my study: I want to evaluate a support group for college students with disabilities. This study (1) evaluates a support group, (2) focuses on young adults (college students are predominantly young adults, so could have similar issues), and (3) uses instruments that may be appropriate for my study.

(b)   What theory or theories (if any) does the author use in this study? How might you apply this theory to your topic of study?

Life-cycle development theory: to understand issues for this population and to develop intervention. Authors point out that younger cancer patients have concerns that are different from older patients.

Group theory: rationale for using standard support group and other group techniques.

Again, both theories are relevant to my study topic and population.

(c)   In a brief paragraph describe *how* the sample was obtained.

Sample was obtained from patients at community hospitals and a cancer center. Social workers explained the group to potential participants and then referred them to the group if they were interested.

NOTE: Actual procedure differed from the initial plan for the study. Authors wanted to find 20 people and conduct a wait-list control group study. They could not find enough people, so they conducted a one-group pretest-posttest design.

Nonprobability sample. All participants received the intervention.

(d)   Include a brief description of the sample (size, gender, race, age, socioeconomic class, special characteristics), paying close attention to the inclusion and representation of people of color, frequently underrepresented in research. (For example, are people of color included in sufficient numbers, or are several groups simply pooled together with only white and nonwhite comparisons reported?)

Sample size is 14, nine women and five men. Race: 12 are white, one each Native American and African American. Ages range from 24 to 34 years old. Nine participants are disabled or unemployed.

Three of 14 people attended three or fewer group sessions and were not included in data analysis.

Small sample, few people of color included.

See article page 134 for more information on demographics.

(e)   What are the major concepts in the study and the variables chosen to represent each concept?

Major concepts.	Variables.
Psychological well-being	tension-anxiety, depression-dejection, anger-hostility, vigor-activity, fatigue-inertia, confusion-bewilderment (subscales on POMS, see below)
Coping	coping responses (from WCCL-R, see below)
Quality of life	physical, psychosocial, medical interaction, marital, sexual problems (subscales on CARES, see below)

(f)   Indicate the specific measures used (operationalization) for each of the major variables in the article that are relevant to your study. Begin with the dependent variables if dependent and independent variables are included. If the article is an evaluation of an intervention, briefly describe the intervention (usually the independent variable).

Dependent Variables:	Measures:
tension-anxiety, depression-dejection, anger-hostility, vigor-activity, fatigue-inertia, confusion-bewilderment	Profile of Mood States (POMS)
coping responses	Cancer Rehabilitation Evaluation System (CARES)
physical, psychosocial, medical interaction, marital, sexual problems	Ways of Coping Checklist (WCCL-R)
Independent Variable:	Structured, six-week, support group intervention (pp. 135-137)

(g)   Describe the method of data collection.

Quantitative:
Participants completed scales prior to beginning the group and again one to two weeks after the group ended. Instruments were mailed to participants for them to complete.

Qualitative:
The researcher was a participant-observer at the group meetings, and made notes during the groups. Researcher also interviewed group participants to ask them what they found helpful about the group.

(h)   Summarize the findings of the study in two or three sentences.

Quantitative results based on scales: Participants indicated an improvement in psychological well-being, but no change in their coping or quality of life. (Because of small sample size, statistical significance is difficult.)

Qualitative results: participants were asked what was helpful about the group. Areas (themes) related to helpfulness identified: shared experiences, meeting people in same age group, group atmosphere, receiving information.

Authors also combined quantitative and qualitative data to assess the group's goals. For specifics, see article page 139.

(i) What will you apply from this study to your own? How might you use its strengths or compensate for its limitations?

Intervention is similar to the intervention I am evaluating, a short-term, structured group.

Intervention uses developmental theory and group theory to explain the rationale for the group and logic for why the group should be effective. Specifically, a younger population of cancer patients faces developmental issues out of "the norm" and may have unique concerns and needs.

My sample size will be small, too, and I may have a similar problem getting enough respondents to have a wait-list control group.

Instruments (POMS and WCCL-R) may be appropriate for my study.

Combines quantitative with qualitative data.

Article does a good job describing the intervention.

Analysis used matched pair t-test (check with Dr. Dietz to see if this will work for my analysis).

Authors recommend a longer intervention (8 weeks) so there is time for an introduction and termination session. I think I will have time to do an 8 week group.

Also, authors recommend a closed-session AND time-limited group.

No control group, so authors have to deal with possible threats to internal validity (maturation).

(2)   For nonempirical articles

These articles will most likely be expository articles: discussions of theory, summaries of many other studies, or general overviews of the topic you are studying. For each article you plan to use, ask yourself the following questions.

Author and Date _____

Title _____

Citation Information _____

_____

(a)   What is the main topic of this article?

(b)   What information does it provide that is helpful for a better understanding of the topic or helpful in the actual design of your study?

SAMPLE FOR NONEMPIRICAL ARTICLE

These articles will most likely be expository articles: discussions of theory, summaries of many other studies, or general overviews of the topic you are studying. For each article you plan to use, ask yourself the following questions.

Author and Date *Fineran, S. & Bennett, L. (1998)*

Title *Teenage Peer Sexual Harassment: Implications for Social Work*

Practice in Education

Citation Information *Social Work (43)1, 55-64*

(a)   What is the main topic of this article?

Sexual harassment. Specifically, peer sexual harassment among youth in school settings. Article discusses history of sexual harassment, reviews empirical literature, and uses theories to assist social workers in school settings.

(b)   What information does it provide that is helpful for a better understanding of the topic or helpful in the actual design of your study?

My study explores reasons why high school students want to, or are forced to, attend alternative schools. This article suggests peer sexual harassment as a reason students perform poorly in school or do not want to attend school.

✓ Defines terms.
✓ Review of literature on peer sexual harassment.
✓ Role of social work.
✓ Theories to help understand sexual harassment.

REMINDER:

When writing the research proposal, the text is written in future tense, indicating what you will be doing. When writing the final research report, you will have completed the study. The report will describe and explain what you have done, so the report will be written in past tense. Be sure to change the tense to indicate that you have completed the study.

(C) Write the INTRODUCTION section

Before you start writing, check with your course instructor for the reference style that she or he expects you to follow. Much social work literature uses the American Psychological Association (APA) reference style.

You will save much time and energy if you use the expected format and style as you conduct the project and write early drafts. We know from experience that it takes less effort now to put the paper into the correct style than to revise it later. The library and your university's writing center can provide style manuals to guide you.

Once you have received feedback from your course instructor, you are ready to write the first draft of the introduction and literature review sections of your paper. We say first draft because as you complete the other steps of your study, you may find more information that you want to include.

The introduction section of your paper should be about one to two pages and address the information below. Refer back to **Section III: The Research Question** for information to include:

- ◆ Scope and significance of the problem or issue
- ◆ Relevance to social work
- ◆ Specification of the research question (purpose of the study)

(D) Write the LITERATURE REVIEW section

(1)   Make a plan for how you will present related literature. What are the main topics you will cover in your review?

Organize the topics in a meaningful way so that your discussion of the literature has a logical flow. Try beginning with broad, general information and move to more specific information. Use an expository article to make a particular point and then an empirical article to provide evidence for that point.

Organizing the literature review is always a difficult process—even for experienced researchers—so don't get discouraged. We have provided an example of an annotated literature review on pages 58 through 63 to help you write your literature review.

Outline your literature review on separate pages.

(2)   Using your outline as a guide, write your review of the literature (minimum of four pages). Use subheadings that match your topics to help the reader follow your outline. At the end of the literature review state your research question again in its final form.

Keep in mind that as you continue through the workbook and the design of your study, you will probably locate other sources that you will include in the final draft of your paper.

Remember that you have an ethical responsibility to cite all your sources properly, to indicate when you are using an author's exact words, and to make it clear when you are paraphrasing an author's ideas. If you are uncertain about proper documentation, ask your instructor for assistance or go to your university's writing center.

Submit the drafts of the Introduction and Literature Review sections to your course instructor along with **Section V: Choosing Your Methodology.**

Annotated Example of a Literature Review

Introduction

[1] Antiretrovirals (ARVs), particularly protease inhibitors, are potent agents in reducing the viral load in HIV-positive individuals. However, these positive effects can be short-lived in many patients if they do not take the antiretroviral medications as prescribed. Poor patient adherence to these drugs can rapidly lead to resistance and negate the benefits of combination therapy. In addition, as a result of poor adherence, public health is threatened as the virus becomes resistant to antiretroviral therapy.

[2] Recent research on adherence to antiretrovirals suggests that adherence rates greater than 90 percent are necessary to maintain suppression of HIV (Patterson et al., 1999). Unfortunately, numerous studies have documented low rates of adherence to antiretroviral medication among HIV-positive individuals (Leslie, 2000). [3] While researchers have sought to determine factors related to adherence among this group, very few efforts have been directed at designing and evaluating approaches to assisting individuals in improving adherence. [2] This area of research is absolutely critical to the development of an effective response to the HIV epidemic (Michael, 2000).

[4] This study seeks to evaluate the effectiveness of a bi-weekly phone counseling approach in increasing adherence to antiretroviral medications among HIV+ persons. [5] The intervention model takes into account individual stages of change readiness and begins the intervention at the patient's level.

Background

HIV in the United States

[6] Due to improved antiretroviral therapies and treatment strategies, death rates and opportunistic infections associated with AIDS have declined since late 1995; however, the estimated total number of persons living with AIDS has steadily increased. According to the most recent HIV/AIDS Surveillance Report, a total of 665,357 persons with AIDS have been reported to the Centers for Disease Control (CDC) through 30 June 1998. Of these, 401,028 (60%) deaths have been reported. This report indicates that the estimated number of persons living with AIDS is currently greater than 264,000 (Centers for Disease Control and Prevention, 1998).

Margin annotations:

[1] Establishes importance of the issue

[2] States value of the study

[3] Indicates what is missing from the literature

[4] States purpose of the study

[5] Introduces theoretical connection (additional text removed for the sake of brevity)

[6] Provides context with historical data

Advances in Antiretroviral Therapy

Several significant advances in the approach to antiretroviral therapy have led to the recently observed changes in the AIDS death rates and incidence of opportunistic infections. Protease inhibitors (PI), a new class of antiretrovirals that attack a different enzyme in the HIV life cycle, are potent agents that can lead to dramatic reductions in the amount of virus in an infected patient's plasma (viral load). Another advance involves the use of combination antiretroviral therapy. As described in the treatment guidelines, it is well established that using a PI *in combination with* two nucleoside analogs can lead to reduced plasma viral loads, decreased viral resistance, decreased opportunistic infections, increased CD4 or T-cells, and improved survival in many patients. However, these positive effects can be short-lived in many patients if they do not take the antiretroviral medications as prescribed (Vanhove et al., 1996). Poor patient adherence to these drugs can rapidly lead to resistance which negates the clinical benefits of combination therapy. Thus, much attention has been directed to issues of adherence for persons taking antiretrovirals.

Adherence

[7] Conceptualization: definition of key terms

[7] Defining adherence. Adherence has become a popular term since it may be viewed as less judgmental. However, the terms "compliance" and "adherence" are used interchangeably in the literature (Mehta et al., 1997). As reviewed by Morris and Schulz (1992) patient medication compliance may be defined as a process or an outcome. The outcome-oriented definition is commonly employed by adherence researchers. This approach focuses on a defined outcome as a result of a patient performing a specific action, such as taking medication. It is quantified by the percentage of time that a patient takes her or his medication as prescribed. Currently there is no accepted minimum percentage level or outcome-oriented definition of medication adherence for patients with HIV.

[8] Prior empirical work

[8] Adherence in chronic illnesses. Rates of adherence with long term medications for chronic conditions have consistently been found to average around 50%, regardless of illness or setting (Donovan & Blake, 1992). Medication adherence is well studied for chronic disease states such as diabetes, hypertension, tuberculosis, mental illness, and others (Morris & Schulz, 1992).

Adherence among HIV+ Patients. Data regarding medication adherence in HIV-infected patients first appeared in the literature in the early 1990s (Samuels et al., 1990). The early studies centered around adherence to single agent antiretroviral regimens involving zidovudine

(Samuels et al., 1990; Morse et al., 1991; Samet et al., 1992; Broers et al., 1994; Wall et al., 1995; Geletko et al., 1996). However, over the past two years there has been renewed interest in evaluating adherence issues in this population due to the increased utilization of combination therapy that requires patients to take complex, multidrug medication regimens with varied dosing schedules. This is a result of, in part, a more complete understanding of viral replication, dynamics, and the development of resistance (Ho, 1996; Mellors et al., 1996). Consideration of practical treatment issues--such as antiretroviral regimens that must be taken indefinitely involving medications that are often times prone to significant adverse effects--has also influenced the renewed interest in evaluating adherence.

  <u>Recent medication adherence studies in HIV patients.</u> Recent medication studies indicate that 21 to 43% of all patients regularly miss doses of their antiretroviral or opportunistic infection prophylaxis medications. Evidence of nonadherence for a substantial group in this population is currently well documented. More disconcerting are the findings that approximately 40% of treated patients showed detectable viral loads. While the survival benefit provided by these multidrug antiretroviral regimens is impressive, recent findings by Paterson and colleagues (1999) indicate that even >95% adherence resulted in viral suppression for only 81% of patients.

Measuring Adherence

[9] Adherence typically has been measured both directly and indirectly (Morris & Schulz, 1992). Direct measurements involve detection of certain chemicals in body fluid levels, whereas indirect measures include prescription refills, pill counts, medication self-reports, and even the subjective impressions of health care providers (cf. Morse et al., 1991). Direct measurements, while objective and less biased, may be influenced by individual patient pharmacokinetics and time of medication dosing. Additionally, these methods do not accurately reflect what activity has taken place over time, are generally impractical in many settings, and often lack established reference ranges relative to specific dosing activity.

[10] Indirect measures such as patient interviews and self-reports are among the more common methods; however, they usually overestimate compliance despite the skill of the interviewer or design of the self-report form (Cramer et al., 1989). Prescription refill data and pill counts may be inaccurate since they do not indicate whether medication was taken at prescribed intervals and because patients may discard their medication before a visit to their physician (Scaler et al.,

[9] Operationalization: Measures used in prior empirical work

[10] Critique of measures

1994). Electronic monitoring is an indirect measure that allows for a more accurate assessment of compliance as compared to pill counts and patient interviews as shown in numerous studies (Pflomm et al., 1997; Wall et al., 1995; Geletko et al., 1996). However, compliance may still be overestimated since it does not verify the exact dose that was removed from the container or if the medication was actually ingested (Scaler et al., 1994).

Measuring adherence in HIV+ patients. A variety of measurement tools have been employed to study medication adherence in HIV-infected patients. Some of these include: questionnaires, diaries, pill count, self report, laboratory/biological markers, antiretroviral plasma assays, physician or study nurse assessments, prescription refill compliance, supervised medication administration, and electronic measuring devices. In a study by Morse et al. (1991) the measure of adherence consisted of nurses' subjective assessments of patient compliance based upon criteria such as appointment-keeping. As shown by concurrent evaluation, and as noted above, most methods greatly overestimate actual medication adherence as compared to electronic monitoring (Pflomm et al., 1997; Wall et al., 1995; Geletko et al., 1996). The majority of studies have utilized a combination of methods to assess medication adherence, a logical approach to measuring adherence since most methods, as discussed above, have inherent limitations.

Efforts to Improve Adherence

[11] Summarizes what is currently known regarding interventions to improve adherence

[11] While it is known that adherence is lower when the regimen is complex and of long duration, requires changes in lifestyle, and is inconvenient and expensive (all factors inherent in antiretroviral medication regimens), there is sparse information regarding the best means of enhancing adherence (Eldred et al., 1997; Urquhart, 1992; Scaler et al., 1994). Most interventions can be categorized as educational, behavioral, or a combination of the two. Educational strategies, involving written and/or verbal communication, are based on an information model of adherence and suggest that patients given sufficient information (regarding the disease, medications, and side effects) will demonstrate increased adherence. Studies of the effectiveness of written information alone have not shown it to be effective in increasing adherence (Mullen et al., 1985). However, a combination of written and verbal information has shown promise, across settings, in increasing adherence and knowledge among adults with hypertension, but with the qualification of specific, focused one-to-one counseling, often provided by a pharmacist (Hussar, 1985;

Zismer et al., 1982; Nessman et al., 1980; Cole & Emmanuel, 1971). Noble (1998) notes the importance of physician techniques such as getting the patient involved, widening the discussion, shifting the responsibility back to the patient, educating and empowering the patient, and encouraging full collaboration.

Behavioral interventions, such as medication calendars, refill reminders (by phone or mail), and special medication containers have also increased adherence rates (Morris & Schulz, 1992). Most promising, however, has been the combination of educational and behavioral interventions.

[12] Critically analyzes findings

[12] The 1996 review of randomized trials of interventions to improve adherence completed by Haynes, McKibbon, and Kanani stands as the most comprehensive review of that literature to date. Of the 15 RCTs that met their rigorous criteria for inclusion, seven interventions were found to increase adherence levels across clinical problems, including hypertension, asthma, streptococcal throat, epilepsy, and schizophrenia. All but one of those seven involved long-term complex interventions, consisting of various combinations of verbal and written instruction, convenience of care (e.g., simplified dosing), involving patients in their care (e.g., blood pressure monitoring), reminders, and reinforcement. However, the authors concluded that although these complex interventions significantly increased adherence levels, the increases were not significant enough to allow individuals to experience the full benefits of their medications, especially significant in the area of antiretroviral adherence.

Only one study was located that utilized an experimental design to evaluate the effectiveness of an intervention to increase adherence to an antiretroviral, ZDV. Sorenson et al. (1998) evaluated eight weeks of onsite dispensing to 25 patients enrolled in a methadone clinic and compared outcomes to those randomly assigned to a usual care group. The researchers found no statistically significant differences in self-report of adherence during the intervention or at the one month follow-up.

In adherence research it is easy to lose track of the ultimate goal beyond improved adherence, that of clinical benefit. Six of the interventions reviewed by Haynes et al. (1996) resulted in clinical improvement, with only four demonstrating improvement in both adherence and clinical outcome, further emphasizing the researchers' point that the increases in adherence were generally not substantial. Likewise, the Sorenson et al. (1998) study found no significant clinical benefit of onsite dispensing (using mean corpuscular volume as an indicator). Haynes et al. (1996) cited the urgent need for testing of further innovations in treatment methods, innovations that "are more likely to occur if investigators join across clinical disciplines to tackle low adherence" (p. 386).

Summary

[13] Near total adherence for individuals taking antiretrovirals is absolutely essential. Unfortunately, only 57-79% of persons taking antiretrovirals achieve adherence levels of 80% more, a level that most clinicians and researchers realize is unacceptable for this population in its fight against HIV. Equally unfortunate is that, constrained by a relatively short time of investigation, the factors related to adherence have not been well-identified. Neither have the few tests of health behavior models been well supported. Even more unfortunate is that evaluations of efforts to improve adherence among HIV+ individuals have been rare.

[14] Utilizing a randomized wait-list control group experimental design in two sites, chosen specifically to test the intervention in settings already providing HIV care (a university-based HIV clinic and a community-based pharmacy specializing in HIV care), we intend to:

(1) provide and evaluate services designed to increase levels of adherence among 50 individuals; and

(2) assess risk factors for nonadherence by examining the link between adherence and sociodemographic variables, disease state and perceived risk and threat of illness, intention to adhere, medication regimen, social supports, substance abuse, and emotional health.

[13] Reviews key points of literature review

[14] Restates purpose of proposed study

Written by Alex Westerfelt, Ph.D., School of Social Welfare and Melinda Lacy, Pharm.D., School of Pharmacy, University of Kansas.

CHOOSING YOUR METHODOLOGY & DEVELOPING A TIME LINE

Having examined the literature, you know some of the methods of study used to explore your topic. Now you must decide the particular method you will use to conduct your own investigation. This workbook allows for four options: survey research, qualitative research, single-subject design research, and program outcomes evaluation.

In most instances, to the extent that you have narrowed and adequately specified your research question, you will have obligated yourself to a particular method of study. If you are uncertain, review your research question. Inherent in most research questions is an indication of the purpose of the research to be undertaken. Remember! Purpose directs method. Ask yourself what the purpose of your study is.

(A) Determine the purpose of your study

Check to see which of the following best applies to your question.

❏ If the purpose of your study is to document the magnitude of a problem or the quantity of various characteristics (for example, how satisfied with services are people, or how many people need a particular service) or determine individual ratings based on scaled measures (for example, parenting skills), then you will use the survey method. Go to **Section VI.**

❏ If the purpose of your study is to gain a deeper understanding from the individual's perspective of how each participant has experienced a particular event or state (for example, homelessness), then qualitative interviewing usually will be your method of choice. This is also true when

NAME: DATE:

RESEARCH QUESTION:

exploring something about which little is known (for example, how terminally ill cancer patients perceive home visits by social work case managers). Go to **Section VII**.

☐   If the purpose of your study is to evaluate how an intervention affects a single client system (individual, family, program, or community), then single-subject design will most likely be your method of choice. Go to **Section VIII**.

☐   If the purpose of your study is to evaluate how an intervention or program affects several clients, then a group design is your method of choice. Go to **Section IX**.

This is not to say there is only one right method for each question. The choice of method depends greatly on the exact specification of what you want to know. Because each research question is unique, we cannot give more specific guidance regarding which method to choose, and we encourage you to talk with your course instructor for further help. Prepare for a discussion with your course instructor by thinking about the purpose of your study and what you have learned from reviewing the literature.

Once you have chosen your method of study, proceed to that section of the workbook.

Write a sentence combining the purpose of your study and the method you have chosen below.

```
PURPOSE OF YOUR STUDY AND METHOD:




```

(B)   Develop your proposed time line

Now, you should plan for implementing your study. On page 68, we provide time frames for conducting a research study as part of a one semester course. You may have more or less time to conduct your study, so plan accordingly.

Enter the dates for each part of your proposed study on page 68.

(C)   Submit proposed study to your course instructor

Submit drafts of the Introduction and Literature Review sections of your paper along with this section (**Section V**) to your course instructor for his/her feedback.

```
COURSE INSTRUCTOR SIGN-OFF:


```

Study Time Line
(suggested time periods for a one semester course)

Literature Review, Research Design, and Sample Design	4 weeks	_____ enter start date above
Instrument Development	2 weeks	_____ start date
Instrument and Data Collection Pilot	2 weeks	_____ start date**
Data Collection	4 weeks	_____ start date
Data Analysis	2 weeks	_____ start date
Prepare Final Report	2 weeks	_____ start date
Submit Final Report		_____ due date

First IRB submission date: _____ *Final IRB approval date:* _____
(Must be prior to ** above)

SURVEY RESEARCH

RECOMMENDED ARTICLE:

Marino, R., Green, R. & Young, E. (1998). Beyond the scientist-practitioner model's failure to thrive: Social workers' participation in agency-based research activities. *Social Work Research, 22*(3), 188-192.

Researchers rely more on survey methods than any other method. With appropriate sampling procedures, researchers utilize survey methods to gather a wealth of information about individuals, families, groups, and communities. Options for the design of survey studies are addressed below. This section of the workbook is intended to guide you through each of the steps necessary to design a survey study.

Now that you have completed a review of the literature, you are ready to develop a research instrument and plan its method of administration.

(A) Translate concepts and variables into measures

REMINDER:

Review your methods text regarding operationalization and measurement.

In your literature review you identified major concepts and variables from other studies and indicated the measures (indicators) chosen for each of them. Now you will develop the indicators for each variable you intend to measure.

In the case of scales that are used in studies and cited in articles, you may have to locate another article that contains the actual items of the scale and includes information about the development and testing of that scale. The other article will be listed in the references of the study article you have

NAME: DATE:

RESEARCH QUESTION:

read. Sometimes you may need to call or write the author to see the actual scale. Some scales are copyrighted and can be used only if a fee is paid for each one used. If you plan to use an existing scale, allow time to find these things out and obtain a copy of the scale.

In addition to what you have found in your literature review, there are other resources available to you. Your agency may have instruments that are available for your use. There are also texts which include multiple scales such as Fischer and Corcoran's (1994) *Measures for Clinical Practice* and Jordan and Franklin's (1995) *Clinical Assessment for Social Workers*. These usually can be found in your library's reference section. For additional suggestions for texts with existing scales, see Rubin and Babbie's (1997) *Research Methods for Social Work*, pages 150-151.

If, on the other hand, you develop your own instrumentation, allow time to share it with others and receive feedback.

(1)   What are the key variables of interest in your study?

Drawing from your literature review, how have others measured each of these?

On the following page, specify each variable, then list the author, date, the specific measure, and, in the case of scales, the scale's validity and reliability.

If the agency has measured these variables before, include those measures or questions here.

VARIABLE AUTHOR/DATE	MEASURE	BRIEF DESCRIPTION	SCALE RELIABILITY/VALIDITY
(1)			
(2)			
(3)			

(2)　Your intended measures

    (a)　Circle the above measures which you plan to use. You may choose more than one. If you do not plan to use any of the measures, go to Part (b). If you plan to use one or more scales, check the original source on each scale, and indicate how much time it will take to complete the measure, either by interview or self-administered.

(b)   If none of the above measures seems appropriate, or if you want to develop measures of your own in addition to conventional measures you have selected, indicate why.

(c)   What measure(s) do you propose?

(d)   Evaluate whether the above measures have a cultural bias in terms of age; race; gender; social class; physical, mental or emotional ability; or sexual orientation. In the case of validated scales, with whom and with what age group have the scales been tested for validity and reliability?

(e)   If creating a scale or composite measure, indicate the time it will take to administer the measures.

(f)   Discuss potential limitations of your measures relative to reliability and validity.

(B) Construct your research questionnaire

REMINDER:
Review your text regarding construction of questionnaires.

You are now ready to construct the questionnaire for your study. The measures you have detailed above will make up part of the questionnaire, but you will probably want to include other items as well. The following questions are intended to help you further develop the questionnaire.

(1)   What other questions would agency staff like to include? Indicate to whom you talked and their ideas.

(2) What other questions would clients like to include? Indicate to whom you talked and their ideas.

(3) Indicate basic, relevant information you wish to collect, such as age, race, gender, or social class.

(4) On separate pages, draft a copy of your questionnaire, including each question word-for-word, in the order you intend to present the items.

(5)   Refine each item on the questionnaire to accomplish the following:

      ❏   For close-ended questions, exhaustive and mutually exclusive responses.
      ❏   No double-barreled questions.
      ❏   No biased items or terms.
      ❏   No leading questions.
      ❏   Clear instructions if questionnaire is to be self-administered.

(6)   Revise your draft so that you can answer "yes" to the following questions, placing a check in the space when you meet the criterion.

      ❏   Is the questionnaire uncluttered?
      ❏   Is it as brief as possible?
      ❏   Is the order of questions appropriate (first questions capture the participant's interest; sensitive questions come later)?
      ❏   Are appropriate "skip" questions used so that people are not asked irrelevant questions?
      ❏   Have you ordered the questions in a way that will be easy for you to analyze and tabulate?
      ❏   Is the language appropriate for the participants?

(7)   Give the questionnaire to two others to critique (your field instructor, other agency staff, peers).

(8)   On a separate page, produce a "clean" version of your questionnaire, incorporating the feedback you received from others.

(9)   Submit your draft questionnaire to your course instructor to approve before you pilot it. Include a synopsis of your research instrument, including the topics it covers. Indicate that you have done so by having the course instructor initial and date here.

COURSE INSTRUCTOR SIGN-OFF:

(C) Plan how to administer your questionnaire

Survey research can be conducted in several ways. You must decide if the questionnaire will be self-administered by the participant or administered by an interviewer who will record the participant's responses. Also, you must decide whether you will distribute the questionnaire in person to the participants or mail it to them.

Complete the following questions. Some questions may not apply to you depending on the method of administration you choose. Simply skip those questions and go to the next set.

If the questionnaire is to be self-administered (as opposed to completed by an interviewer) and distributed by the researcher or an assistant (as opposed to distributed by mail):

(1)   When, where, and how will the questionnaire be distributed? By whom? Will it be distributed to individuals or groups? Justify your choices.

(2) List the information that the person administering the instrument will give to the participant prior to beginning the questionnaire.

(3) Will the questionnaire be anonymous or confidential? Include your rationale for the option you have chosen.

(4)   What are the conditions for questionnaire completion and return? Completed on the spot or returned later? If later, will each one be dropped off by the participant or picked up by someone? Final date for returns? Plans for follow-up of unreturned questionnaires? Justify your choices.

(5)   What are your plans to enhance your response rate?

(6)   Describe any compensation to the participants for their time and expenses and the procedure for compensation. (Federal rules on research stipulate that you cannot offer incentives to participants, but you can compensate them for their time.)

(7)   What are your procedures for handling a situation where an individual starts but does not complete the questionnaire?

If the questionnaire is to be self-administered and distributed by mail:

(1)   Will the questionnaire be anonymous or confidential? Include your rationale for the option you have chosen.

(2)   On separate pages, outline a cover letter including the following points:

—persuasive introduction regarding importance of the questionnaire

—purpose of the study

—who is sponsoring the research

—explanation of how the sample was selected

—statement that participation is voluntary and will not affect services for which the participant is eligible

—assurance of anonymity or confidentiality

—estimated time for completion of the questionnaire

—directions for return of the questionnaire

—cutoff date for return of the questionnaire

(3)   On a separate page, write your cover letter.

(4)   Indicate whether you plan to use stamped return envelopes or business reply envelopes and why.

(5)   Indicate your plans and dates regarding follow-up mailings, if any. What is the estimated total cost for your mailing?

(6)   What are your plans to enhance the response rate?

(7)   Describe any compensation to the participants for their time and expenses and the procedure for compensation. (Federal rules on research stipulate that you cannot offer incentives to participants, but you can compensate them for their time.)

If the questionnaire will be completed by interview:

(1)   When and where will the interviews be conducted? By whom?

(2)   What are your plans to enhance your response rate; i.e., to persuade people to agree to be interviewed?

(3)   Describe any compensation to the participants for their time and expenses and the procedure for compensation. (Federal rules on research stipulate that you cannot offer incentives to participants, but you can compensate them for their time and other expenses they incur, such as travel and child care.)

(4)   What are your procedures for handling a situation where an individual starts but does not complete the interview?

(D) Pilot your research instrument and plan for data collection

The validity and reliability of your questionnaire can be greatly enhanced by piloting it prior to your actual data collection. This also helps you anticipate any problems related to administration. You must obtain prior approval from agency personnel before piloting the instrument with clients. Coordinate this through your course instructor and field instructor.

(1) Pilot your instrument, making conditions as similar as possible to those you expect during data collection. Include agency staff, classmates, and clients of the agency who would not eventually receive the questionnaire.

(2) Indicate with whom you piloted your instrument and the results of the pilots. Discuss questions that were problematic for people, variations in length of time to administer, logistical problems regarding where and how the interviews were conducted, and any problems with administering the consent form.

(3) Indicate below the changes you will make in the administration of your study, based on the results of your pilot. Obtain your course instructor's approval and have him or her initial and date here.

(4) Now revise your questionnaire and have your course instructor approve the final version. Indicate that you have done so by having him or her initial and date here.

COURSE INSTRUCTOR SIGN-OFF:

(E)   Write the METHODS section

Again, this will be a first draft of this section of your paper. As you proceed through the following steps, you may return to this section and make revisions. This section will vary in length according to how many measures you have chosen. You can expect this section of the paper to be roughly two to three pages. It should include the following information:

♦ Each major variable, starting with the dependent variable, if applicable
♦ The chosen measure(s) for each variable and use in prior studies
♦ Validity and reliability of each measure
♦ A brief overview of pilot efforts
♦ Details of plans for administration of the questionnaire

(F)   Data collection

Data collection should follow the plan you set out in this section. Once you have completed data collection, you will revise the methods section to report how you actually collected the data.

QUALITATIVE RESEARCH

RECOMMENDED ARTICLE:

Siegel, D. H. (1993). Open adoption of infants: Adoptive parents' perceptions of advantages and disadvantages. *Social Work, 38*(1), 15-23.

The goal of qualitative research is to study a problem in depth and in detail from the perspective of the research participant in order to understand the meanings people give to situations and experiences. In qualitative research the data are textual rather than numeric.

Qualitative studies are similar to social work case studies and seek to understand what people believe and feel about a particular problem, situation, or program. Qualitative studies help us understand a problem or situation by focusing on a small number of people's experiences. Program evaluations, needs assessments, and client satisfaction studies can be conducted using qualitative methods as well. Data for qualitative studies are most often collected through interviewing, by observation, and from existing documents such as agency documents and newspaper articles. Although there are several methods for collecting qualitative data, we focus solely on interviewing with individuals or groups.

Qualitative is not easier than quantitative just because you don't have to "do" statistics! After completing the interviews, the researcher must analyze and synthesize verbal rather than numerical data. Qualitative analysis requires rigorous analytical thinking and the ability to convey that in written form.

Keep in mind: The perspective of the research participant is of utmost importance and relevance to a qualitative study.

REMINDER:

Review a text devoted to qualitative methods. A general research text may not provide enough information to help you conduct a good qualitative study.

NAME: DATE:

RESEARCH QUESTION:

(A)   Develop the interview agenda (your research instrument)

(1)   Review your research question and your rationale for deciding to conduct a qualitative study. Remember, qualitative studies are exploratory in nature. Refer to your literature review to remind yourself what others studying your topic found. Write here the specific topics they included in their studies.

(2)   Decide whether you will conduct semi-structured or structured interviews. (We do not recommend unstructured interviewing for novice researchers.) Indicate your rationale for your choice.

(3)   Develop a list of demographic and other general information you want to collect for each participant (e.g., age, race, gender, or social class). List these below.

(4)   Brainstorm the topics you want to cover to answer your research question. List them below.

(5)   Ask your field instructor, other agency staff, clients, and your peers for their suggestions regarding topics to include in the interviews. List to whom you talked and their suggestions.

(6)   From your research topics, develop open-ended questions that will obtain information to answer your research questions. Don't worry about the order of the questions at this point, but you should pay special attention to the wording. Questions should be focused, yet broad enough to allow the participants to share their perspectives. Avoid biases of age; race; gender; social class; physical, mental, or emotional ability; or sexual orientation. Use a separate page to write your questions.

(7)   Now, add "probes" to each of the main questions that you have developed. Probes will provide guidance for the interviewer (even if you are the only interviewer).

(8)   Draft your interview agenda on separate pages, putting your questions and probes into a format that follows a logical order. Questions should move from general to specific and from less sensitive to more sensitive topics. The interview format should make sense to your participants *and* allow you to stay focused while collecting data.

Circulate the draft of your interview agenda to the people who helped you generate questions and to other individuals as well. Obtain their feedback and revise your interview agenda. List here with whom you talked, their titles or roles, and the feedback they gave.

NAME:	FEEDBACK:

(9)   Now is the time to share your interview agenda with your course instructor for approval and feedback. Indicate that you have done so by having him or her initial and date here.

COURSE INSTRUCTOR SIGN-OFF:

(B)   Plan how to conduct interviews

REMINDER:
Refer to a qualitative methods text for information about conducting in-depth interviews with individuals or in a group setting (focus groups).

(1)   Indicate whether you will conduct individual or group interviews. Give the rationale for your choice.

(2)   How and where will the interviews be scheduled?

(3)   How will you record the data? What will you need to conduct the interview? Tape recording with an audio cassette recorder and having your tapes transcribed verbatim is one method. However, you may not have the resources for this. (One hour of interview time takes at least three to four hours to transcribe.) Other means of recording qualitative interview data include (1) taping with partial transcribing, (2) taping and later taking notes while listening to the tapes, and (3) taking extensive notes during and after the interviews when recording is not possible. These notes are commonly referred to as field notes.

(4)   Indicate who will conduct the interviews. If there is more than one interviewer, how will you prepare the interviewers so that the interviews are conducted consistently? Specify the training and supervision interviewers will receive.

(5) Describe any compensation to the participants for their time and expenses and the procedure for compensation. (Federal rules on research stipulate that you cannot offer incentives to participants, but you can compensate them for their time and other expenses they incur, such as travel and child care.)

(6)   List the information you will give to the participant just prior to the start of the interview. (Remember to also have the participant read and sign the consent form prior to the interview.)

Write the above information into a script that the interviewer can read to participants before beginning the interviews.

(7)   What are your procedures for handling a situation where an individual starts but does not complete the interview?

(C) Pilot your interview agenda and plan for data collection

Piloting your interview can help you identify and remedy potential problems in data collection. **You must obtain approval from IRB and agency personnel before piloting your interview with clients.** Coordinate this through your course instructor and field instructor.

(1) Pilot your interview agenda making conditions as similar as possible to those you expect during data collection. You may interview agency staff, classmates, or clients who would not eventually be interviewed.

(2) Indicate with whom you piloted the interview and how long the interview took; include their feedback. Add your own ideas regarding what you think worked well and what you would like to change.

(3) Revise your interview agenda using your experience and the feedback from the participants with whom you piloted the instrument. Obtain final approval of the interview agenda from your field instructor and course instructor. Indicate you have done so by having them initial and date here.

> COURSE INSTRUCTOR SIGN-OFF:

(D) Write the METHODS section

In the first draft of this section (roughly two to three pages), you should include the following:

◆ How you developed the interview agenda
◆ Whether you will conduct individual or group interviews
◆ How you plan to record the data
◆ Who will conduct the interviews and how they will be trained
◆ Results of your pilot efforts

(E) Data collection

Data collection should follow the plan you set out in this section. Once you have completed data collection, you will revise the methods section to report how you actually collected the data.

SINGLE-SUBJECT DESIGN RESEARCH

RECOMMENDED ARTICLE:

Cooper, M. (1990). Treatment of a client with obsessive-compulsive disorder. *Social Work Research and Abstracts,* (June), 26-31. (In the article the Y-axes of the graphs in Figures 1, 2, and 3 are labeled incorrectly. The Y-axes should read "Number," "Minutes," and "Percentage," respectively.)

Single-subject design is also referred to as single-system design, reflecting its applicability to any client system—a single individual, a single family, a single program, a single community. We assume that most students utilizing this design will choose a single individual as the client system, and we have developed the material with that in mind. It is not difficult, however, to adapt and complete this section with a different client system in mind, and we encourage you not to overlook other client systems when considering your options.

Single-subject research is a frequently utilized method of evaluating one's practice. Its implementation parallels many of the activities of good practice. It allows you to evaluate your practice (research) while at the same time it provides a means for facilitating the intervention process (practice).

Single-subject design is inherently a causal study asking whether an intervention is effective. As such, it requires the researcher to be aware of the significant internal and external validity limitations of the design. We strongly encourage you to review this aspect of single-subject design as you plan your study.

This section of the workbook is intended to guide you through the steps necessary to design a single-subject study. First you must determine whether your client is willing to participate in your research study. Review a copy of the consent form with the client. (The consent form is developed in **Section XI**.) Be sure that your client does not feel pressured to participate and understands that refusal to participate will not affect receipt of or eligibility for agency services.

REMINDER:

Review single-subject design in a methods text.

NAME: DATE:

RESEARCH QUESTION:

(A)   Translate concepts and variables into measures

REMINDER:

Review your methods text regarding operationalization and measurement.

In your literature review you identified major concepts and variables from other studies and indicated the measures (indicators) chosen for each of them. Now you will specify the indicators for each variable you intend to measure.

In single-subject design studies, the dependent variable is the target goal chosen by the client and worker. We assume you have discussed with your client what target goals he or she is interested in pursuing, and that your literature review reflects material on such goals. Keep in mind that more than one target goal may be chosen.

There are three broad categories of sources for finding measures: questions or scales currently used by the agency, questions or scales you find in the literature, and your own creations. One advantage of the literature review you did earlier is that it will give you a sense of how others have defined and measured outcomes relative to the issues your intervention addresses.

In the case of scales that are used in studies and cited in articles, you may have to locate another article that contains the actual items of the scale and includes information about the development and testing of that scale. The other article will be listed in the references of the study article you read.

Sometimes you may need to call or write the author to see the actual scale. Some scales are copyrighted and can be used only if a fee is paid for each one used. If you plan to use an existing scale, allow time to find these things out and obtain a copy of the scale.

In addition to what you have found in your literature review, there are other resources available to you. Your agency may have instruments that are available for your use. There are also texts which include multiple scales such as Fischer and Corcoran's (1994) *Measures for Clinical Practice* and Jordan and Franklin's (1995) *Clinical Assessment for Social Workers*. These usually can be found in your library's reference section. For more suggestions for texts on existing scales, see Rubin and Babbie's (1997) *Research Methods for Social Work*, pages 150-151.

If, on the other hand, you develop your own instrumentation, allow time to share it with others and receive feedback.

(1)   What is (are) the dependent variable(s) (outcomes) you are considering?

(2)   Drawing from your literature review, how have others measured each of these?

Specify each outcome variable, then list the author, date, the specific measure, a brief description of it, and, in the case of scales, the scale's validity and reliability.

If the agency has measured these variables before, include those measures or questions here.

OUTCOME AUTHOR/DATE	MEASURE	BRIEF DESCRIPTION	SCALE RELIABILITY/VALIDITY
(1)			
(2)			
(3)			

(3)   Consider the time frame of your study. For which of the measures above is it realistic to expect measurable change to occur within that time frame?

(4)   Your intended measures

(a)   Which of the above measures do you plan to use and why? You may choose more than one. (If you do not plan to use any of the measures, go to Part b.) If you plan to use one or more scales, check the original source on each scale, and indicate how much time it will take to complete the measure, either by interview or if self-administered. Go to (e).

(b)   If none of the above measures seems appropriate, or if you want to develop measures of your own in addition to conventional measures you have selected, indicate why.

(c)   What measure(s) do you propose?

(d)   If creating a scale or composite measure, indicate the time it will take to administer the measures.

(e)   Evaluate whether the above measures have a cultural bias in terms of age; race; gender; social class; physical, mental or emotional ability; or sexual orientation. In the case of validated scales, with whom and with what age group have the scales been tested for validity and reliability?

(f)   Discuss potential limitations of your measures relative to reliability and validity.

(5)   Other considerations for your measures

    (a)   Regardless of the measure(s) you have chosen, what will be your data source? Some of your options include using available records, doing interviews, direct observation, and self-reporting (including the use of logs and journals).

    (b)   Who will be responsible for collecting the data? What is the potential for reactivity, obtrusiveness, and social desirability biases?

(c)   Consider each of the following questions to finalize your choice of measures:

✓ To what extent are the measures sensitive to small, short-term changes?
✓ Are or can the indicators be phrased positively?
✓ For the target goals, will you measure frequency, duration, magnitude, or a combination?
✓ How have you triangulated the target goal measures?

(6)   Specify what your intervention will be (location, specific activities, duration, frequency).

(B) Identify the specific single-subject design

Your choice of design will depend on what is practical in your agency and with your client, the nature of the intervention (varying intensity, multiple components, irreversible effects) and the chosen target goals.

(1)   Graph

Sketch out a simple graph of an AB design. Mark the X axis with the range of scores for the selected target goal and the Y axis with the intended observation points. Draw a vertical line across the Y axis at the point where you intend to begin the intervention, demarcating the baseline and intervention phases.

(2)   Baseline phase

❑   Do you have enough measurement points that a stable baseline can be established (five to ten points)?

❑   Can you use retrospective data for construction of the baseline?

❑   Can you use multiple baselines, either for different target goals or with different clients?

(3)   Intervention phase

❑   Do you intend to withdraw the intervention for some period of time and then provide it again (an ABAB design)? Indicate when and how on the graph.

❑   Do you have an intervention that will be offered in changing intensity (an $AB^1B^2B^3$ design)? Explain and add to the graph.

❑   Do you have an intervention with several components (an ABCD design)? Specify on your graph.

❑   If the intervention seems to be having a negative impact, what is your plan? Indicate it below.

(4)   Sketch out your revised design.

(5)   Would it be possible to do more than one single-subject study; i.e., use the same design with more than one client? Explain.

(6)   Indicate the limitations relative to internal validity. (See pages 125-126 for a review of threats to internal validity.)

(7)   Indicate the limitations relative to external validity.

(C) Write the METHODS section

Again, this will be a first draft of this section because, as you proceed through the other steps, you may return and make revisions. This section will vary in length according to how many measures you have chosen. It should include (roughly one to two pages) the following information:

◆ Dependent variables (the target goals) and the client's input
◆ The chosen measure(s) for each variable and use in prior studies
◆ The validity and reliability of each measure
◆ The independent variable (the intervention)
◆ Details on the chosen design, rationale, and limitations

(D) Data collection

Data collection should follow the plan you set out in this section. Once you have completed data collection, you will revise the methods section to report how you actually collected the data.

NOTE:

*Because single-subject designs use an "N of 1," you do not need to complete **Section X** of the workbook (Sample Design), and you should disregard references to the sample when writing the final report in **Section XIII**. You should, however, give a brief synopsis of the client situation and the circumstances that led to that person's choice of goals. Proceed to **Section XI**.*

COURSE INSTRUCTOR SIGN-OFF:

OUTCOMES EVALUATION

RECOMMENDED ARTICLE:

Roberts, C., Piper, L., Denny, J., & Cuddeback, G. (1997). A support group intervention to facilitate young adults' adjustment to cancer. *Health and Social Work, 22,* 133-141.

Outcomes evaluation is one type of program evaluation. Evaluating the extent to which a program or intervention results in its intended outcomes has become increasingly important as more funders have begun requiring outcomes evaluations as a part of program funding. However, outcomes evaluation has its own intrinsic rewards. Programs can benefit simply from the process of designing an evaluation as providers take the time to consider the "match" between their services and the intended outcomes. What can we realistically expect to happen as a result of this program? This is often referred to as the logic or rationale behind a program, and evaluators will sometimes speak in terms of a "logic model."

For example, objectives for a therapeutic arts program in a juvenile detention facility included the reduction of aggressive behaviors, and in the long run, less recidivism. But should an arts program meeting two hours a week for ten weeks be expected to have these results? The providers realized that such a limited experience in the context of so many influences in a teen's life was unlikely to have a major impact on whether the teen committed future delinquent offenses. Further, as the program providers explained the rationale behind their program, they fully expected that the program, if successful, might initially *increase* acting out behaviors of youth as they began to confront issues in their lives. Simply the *process* of designing an evaluation of their program was immensely helpful to them as they had to think through the rationale behind their intervention (the logic) and what they sought to accomplish (outcomes) with it.

✓ Explicating the basis for an intervention and clarifying the link between the intervention and program objectives answers the questions of why we can expect consumers to change after receiving the intervention and in what ways. In this

---

NAME: DATE:

RESEARCH QUESTION:

section we will guide you through the process of specifying the **logic model** behind your intervention.

✓ The next task involves developing a way in which we can demonstrate that the observed change is a result of the intervention and not other factors in the consumers' lives (commonly known as internal validity). This is the task of **research design**, and in this section we provide three different designs commonly used to evaluate programs (one group pretest-posttest, comparison group, and control group design) and guide you through the process of choosing one for your design.

You may remember from your research class that the one group pretest-posttest design offers virtually no internal validity and thus, really does not answer whether observed changes are a result of the intervention or other factors. We include the design here, however, because often, given the constraints of time and resources facing students in field settings, this design is the only feasible one. It is of value nonetheless as it still requires completion of the tasks of specifying the link between intervention and objectives, developing outcome measures, and planning data collection procedures.

✓ The third task in this outcomes evaluation is to specify the **program outcomes** and their measures. Sometimes programs have stated objectives that lend themselves more easily to the development of outcome measures. Other times, when the objectives are more general or unwritten, the development of outcomes takes more thought. We take you through the various considerations necessary in constructing solid outcome measures.

✓ The final step in this section is development of a plan for when and how the data will be collected. We provide a series of questions to help you incorporate the various considerations necessary for specifying your **data collection procedures**.

At the end of this section on pages 132-133, we provide an example of how each set of questions is answered for the evaluation of a program to improve adherence to a medication regimen.

(A)   Developing the rationale for the intervention: a logic model

(1)   Describe the intervention in terms of targeted problems, services delivered (type, frequency, and duration), who provides the services, and where the services are provided.

(2)   What are the goals of the intervention?

(3)   What is the rationale linking the intervention with those goals? Another way to think of this is to imagine you are explaining to a friend why doing this (the intervention) should result in accomplishing the goals of the program.

(B) Choosing a design

(1)   Can you *randomly assign* some participants to a group who will receive the intervention specified above and others to either a group that will receive an alternative treatment (in essence comparing the relative effectiveness of the two treatments) or to a waiting list group who will receive the treatment after the first group has finished the program?

        If yes, then you can conduct a control group design, a true experimental design, and you should consult your research methods text for a review of that design. Proceed to (4).

        If no, then proceed to the next question.

(2)   Can you find a similar group to those individuals receiving treatment and gather the same information from them over the same period of time as your treatment group?

        If yes, then you can conduct a comparison group design, sometimes referred to as a nonequivalent control group design, a quasi-experimental design, and you should consult your research methods text for a review of that design. Proceed to (4).

        If no, then proceed to the next question.

(3)   If you cannot do either of the above, your last alternative is to conduct a one group pretest-posttest design, and you should consult your research methods text for a review of that design.

(4)   Draw a diagram of your study design, using standard notation for group designs.

Your Design Type: _____

(C) Choosing a sample and assigning groups

(1)   It is important to make a distinction between sample selection and group assignment. Students often confuse *random selection* (which has to do with sample selection) with *random assignment* (which has to do with how a treatment and control group are formed *after* a sample has been selected).

Regardless of which design you are using, you must decide how you will select your sample of program participants. In some cases the number of program participants is small enough that you will choose to study all of them, in effect making your study sample the same as your study population, the group to whom you can generalize your study findings. In other cases, the number of consumers served will be too large for inclusion of all in your sample, and you will have to select a group of them. The larger group becomes the study population from which you will select a study sample.

If you plan to conduct a one group pretest-posttest design, at this point you should complete **Section X** on Sample Design and turn to (D) in this section.

If you plan to conduct a control group design, skip to (3).

(2)   If you plan to conduct a comparison group design, you will in essence need to choose two samples: those who receive the intervention and those who do not. If you have consulted your research text, you know that the credibility of this design relies upon the extent to which you can demonstrate that your comparison group is very similar to your treatment group.

For example, if you were to compare juvenile offenders receiving a therapeutic arts program to offenders in another facility without such a program, you would need to demonstrate that the groups were similar, but in what ways? To answer this question, the researcher draws on his or her knowledge of the literature relative to the factors that have been shown to influence the outcomes you intend to measure. If the arts program seeks to improve participants' abilities to express anger appropriately, the researchers would need to ensure that the two groups were equivalent on the factors that are related to this outcome so that they could rule those factors out as rival explanations for group differences at the end of the study.

In other words, if they found that the treatment group was better able to express anger appropriately at the end of the study as compared to the comparison group, they would not want someone to dispute their findings by noting that the comparison group was different to begin with. An example of this would be if the juvenile offenders receiving treatment were at a minimum security facility, and the juvenile offenders in the comparison group were at a maximum security facility. One could argue that the reason the treatment group fared better on expressing anger appropriately was that they were a less violent group to begin with, or at the least their offenses were much less serious, noting that offense type is often correlated to impulse and anger control. Difference in offense types then becomes a rival to treatment as the explanation for finding differences in anger expression between the two groups.

This is the primary reason researchers often employ the strategy of matching when forming comparison groups. It is an attempt to achieve equivalency of the groups being studied. Unfortunately, we can seldom match participants on all of the characteristics we might worry about as potential rivals (threats) to our findings. This is because such data are often not available, but also because there are only so many combinations of characteristics we can manage at one time. Random assignment remains the only way to contend that the groups are equivalent, and even it is limited when the sample to be divided is small.

The resolution to this problem that is most often used by researchers is to use demographic characteristics—information that is usually available—as proxy measures for the comparability of the two groups. If you can demonstrate that your groups are similar in terms of demographics (age, race, gender, etc.), because other characteristics are often linked to demographic differences, people will be willing to consider that other factors linked to your outcome are likely to be similar in the two groups. Of course, if there are unmeasured but obvious differences between the two groups in spite of demographic similarities (offense type in the example above), you should not choose that group as a comparison group.

Given these considerations, what populations do you think might provide an equivalent comparison group for your treatment group? List them below.

(3)   Consider those factors that might influence your program outcomes. Would any of the groups listed above *obviously* differ from your treatment group on any of these characteristics? If so, it is probably not a good choice. Consider, also, that whatever group becomes your comparison group, they will need to be available for data collection of the same type and at the same times as your treatment group.

Now you should complete **Section X** on Sample Design once for your treatment group and a second time for your comparison group. Then turn to (D) in this section.

(4)   If you plan to conduct a control group design, you must randomly assign the individuals in your sample to separate groups, usually a group that receives the treatment you are studying and a group that receives either an alternative treatment or a group that is placed on a waiting list to receive services at a later date. The assumption of random assignment is that you will have created two groups whose participants are similar to each other on all characteristics. This assumption is easily violated in small samples.

For example, imagine a sample of 20 people randomly split into two groups. The assumption is that the numbers of males and females in one group will be the same in the other group, that the age groupings in one group will be the same as those in the other group, that the variation in attitudes in one group will be just the same in the other group, and so on. However, probability theory tells us that with only 20 people in our sample, it is quite possible that the two groups will not be entirely equivalent in these areas. Thus, it is necessary to gather and present basic demographic and baseline information about the two groups to consider the extent to which they are actually similar to each other.

More information on this idea of equivalency between groups is given in (2) above, and you are encouraged to read it now.

On what variables can you compare your groups?

Now you should complete **Section X** on Sample Design and then turn to (D).

(D) Issues of internal validity

Regardless of the design you have chosen, there will be limitations to your ability to demonstrate that the intervention is responsible for positive changes in your treatment group. These are known as threats to internal validity, and they are discussed in any research text. Because students typically have difficulty applying these threats to particular studies, we present them below in lighter fashion. Some apply only to group designs rather than single subject designs, so do not try to apply all of them without consideration.

(1)   If your study is longitudinal, indicate your ideas for trying to reduce the number of dropouts in your study (attrition, experimental mortality).

(2)   Indicate below each relevant threat and your plans to address that threat. Depending on your design type, you may not be able to do anything to eliminate or reduce a potential threat, but you should at least recognize how it limits your conclusions.

Threats to Internal Validity

The Grandma Factor
- How do we know the changes we see are a result of our efforts and not Grandma's?
- How do we know the changes we see are a result of our efforts and not the holiday spirit?
- This is known as the threat of **history**: extraneous events (potentially influential) that happen at the same time as treatment.

Time Heals All Wounds
- How do we know the changes we see are a result of our efforts and not just the 6 month cycle of depression?
- How do we know the changes we see are a result of our efforts and not just the passage of time?
- This is known as the threat of **maturation** (and also, passage of time): changes over time that have nothing to do with the treatment, but nonetheless affect the results.

Practice Makes Perfect
- How do we know the changes we see are a result of our efforts and not just a result of the fact that people got a chance to practice how to answer the questions (pretest)?
- How do we know the changes we see are a result of our efforts and not just a result of the fact that people know they are being observed or that they will be measured (reactivity effect)?
- This is known as a **testing** threat to internal validity: the effect a pretest has on how people do later on some posttest treatment measure.

To Err Is Human
- How do we know the changes we see are a result of our efforts and not a result of poorly developed measures?
- How do we know the changes we see are a result of our efforts and not a function of using a different pretest and posttest that are not really equal or comparable?
- How do we know the changes we see are a result of our efforts and not a result of inconsistent ratings criteria from pretest to posttest or from one observer to another?
- This is known as an **instrumentation** threat: the effect of errors in measurement on our results.

More Threats to Internal Validity

The Law of Averages

- How do we know the changes we see are a result of our efforts and do not simply reflect the fact that we got most people on a really bad day, got them at their worst, and so later, at the posttest, when several of them were no longer at their worst, on average for the group things are better, but it had absolutely nothing to do with us?

- This is known as **statistical regression** (or regression to the mean): some change for the better will occur whenever we start with people at their worst, just because of the natural ebb and flow of struggles.

Choose Wisely

- How do we know the changes we see are a result of our efforts and not a result of who we studied?

- How do we know the changes we see are a result of our efforts and not a result of simply working with people who were highly motivated to change?

- This threat is known as a **selection bias**: the extent to which a treatment group is not comparable to a nontreatment group.

Dropouts

- How do we know the changes we see are a result of our efforts and not a function of the fact that everyone who did not benefit from our help, dropped out of the study, so our results are based only on those we did help?

- This threat to internal validity is known as **experimental mortality** or **attrition**: the rate at which people drop out of an intervention study before it is finished.

Copycat and Tattletale

- And what about those times when we *don't* find our help to be beneficial? Could something else explain *that*?

- When the ones we work with improve, but not any more than those we didn't work with.

- Maybe those we didn't work with got the same sort of thing somewhere else; from copycats, so to speak.

- Maybe those we didn't work with are chums of those we did work with, and they got all our nuggets of wisdom from their buds; tattletales so to speak.

- This threat is known as **diffusion** (tattletale) or **imitation** (copycat) of treatment — when groups to be compared really aren't so different relative to the services they are receiving.

(E)   Developing outcome measures

Once you have identified the intended program outcomes, the next step is to specify the ways in which those outcomes will be measured. How will you know the intended changes occurred? What will be the evidence of change?

There are three broad categories of sources for finding measures: questions or scales currently used by the agency, questions or scales you find in the literature, and your own creations. One advantage of the literature review you did earlier is that it will give you a sense of how others have defined and measured outcomes relative to the issues your intervention addresses.

In the case of scales that are used in studies and cited in articles, you may have to locate another article that contains the actual items of the scale and includes information about the development and testing of that scale. The other article will be listed in the references of the study article you read. Sometimes you may need to call or write the author to see the actual scale. Some scales are copyrighted and can be used only if a fee is paid for each one used. If you plan to use an existing scale, allow time to find these things out and obtain a copy of the scale.

In addition to what you have found in your literature review, there are other resources available to you. Your agency may have instruments that are available for your use. There are also texts which include multiple scales such as Fischer and Corcoran's (1994) *Measures for Clinical Practice* and Jordan and Franklin's (1995) *Clinical Assessment for Social Workers*. These usually can be found in your library's reference section. For additional suggestions for texts on existing scales, see Rubin and Babbie's (1997) *Research Methods for Social Work*, pages 150-151.

If, on the other hand, you develop your own instrumentation, allow time to share it with others and receive feedback.

(1)   What is (are) the dependent variable(s) (outcomes) you are considering?

(2)   Drawing from your literature review, how have others measured each of these?

Specify each outcome variable, then list the author, date, the specific measure, a brief description of it, and, in the case of scales, the scale's validity and reliability.

If the agency has measured these variables before, include those measures or questions here.

OUTCOME AUTHOR/DATE	MEASURE	BRIEF DESCRIPTION	SCALE RELIABILITY/VALIDITY
(1)			
(2)			
(3)			

(3)   Consider the time frame of your study. For which of the measures above is it realistic to expect measurable change to occur within that time frame?

(4)   Your intended measures

    (a)   Which of the above measures do you plan to use and why? You may choose more than one. (If you do not plan to use any of the measures, go to Part b.) If you plan to use one or more scales, check the original source on each scale, and indicate how much time it will take to complete the measure, either by interview or if self-administered. Go to (e).

(b) If none of the above measures seems appropriate, or if you want to develop measures of your own in addition to conventional measures you have selected, indicate why.

(c) What measure(s) do you propose?

(d) If creating a scale or composite measure, indicate the time it will take to administer the measures.

(e)   Evaluate whether the above measures have a cultural bias in terms of age; race; gender; social class; physical, mental or emotional ability; or sexual orientation. In the case of validated scales, with whom and with what age group have the scales been tested for validity and reliability?

(f)   Discuss potential limitations of your measures relative to reliability and validity.

Now you are ready to construct your research questionnaire and develop a plan for its administration. Complete (C) and (D) in **Section VI** on Survey Research.

Following completion of those sections, you will have all the information you need to complete a workplan similar to the one that follows.

Logic Model for the QUEST Program

Program: QUEST
Provide bi-weekly telephone counseling to HIV+ individuals taking antiretroviral (ARV) medications.

Objectives:
(1) To improve adherence to medication.
(2) To improve physical health.

Logic:
Recent research on adherence to ARVs suggests that adherence rates greater than 90% are necessary to maintain suppression of HIV. Numerous studies have found that rates of adherence are generally low (40%-60%) because of the difficulty people have in adapting a complex medication regimen to their daily routine. If individuals can be helped to develop ways of adapting the medication regimen to their lifestyle rather than the other way around, and if they can be supported during the time required to develop a "habit of adherence," then adherence rates should improve.

Design:
Comparison group design:

$$\begin{array}{ccc} O_1 & X & O_2 \\ \hline O_3 & & O_4 \end{array}$$

Samples:
Experimental group: 25 randomly chosen patients from 217 outpatients at an HIV clinic at hospital X who are participants in the QUEST program.
Comparison group: 25 randomly chosen patients from 150 outpatients at an HIV clinic at hospital Y who are receiving standard case management services.
Experimental and comparison group are similar in that the clinics at both hospitals serve similar groups with respect to race, gender, and public vs. private pay.

Hypotheses:
(1) At the end of three months, adherence will be higher for individuals who receive the intervention as compared to individuals in the comparison group.
(2) At the end of three months physical health status will be better for individuals who receive the intervention as compared to individuals in the comparison group.

Outcomes	Measures	Source of Data	When Collected	Where Collected	How Collected
Participants will demonstrate increases in adherence levels.	Number of doses taken as prescribed in each of past three days	Participant	Start of intervention (pretest) and end of intervention (posttest)	At home visit for pretest	Interview
	Number of pills left in prescription bottle on specific date compared to number that should be left	Pill count by interviewer		At home visit for posttest	Interview
Participants will have better physical health.	Lab results: CD4 counts Lab results: Viral load	Physician or Nurse (with signed consent)	Pretest and posttest	By mail	Questionnaire

Independent Variables	Measures	Source of Data	When Collected	Where Collected	How Collected
Intervention	Number of phone calls completed and home visits	Social workers	Bi-weekly	Office	Case records
Race	White (not Hispanic), Afr. Am., Hispanic or Latino, Asian, Amer. Ind., Other (specify)	Participant	Pretest	Home visit	Interview
Gender	Male, Female	Participant	Pretest	Home visit	Interview
Health Insurance	Private, Medicaid, Medicare, Ryan White Funds	Participant	Pretest and posttest	Home visit	Interview
Social Support	Number of persons living with participant	Participant	Pretest and posttest	Home visit	Interview

SAMPLE DESIGN

REMINDER:

Review sample design in a methods text. Pay close attention to the difference between probability and nonprobability sampling methods. Within each of those two broad types of sampling methods, review the different types of samples that can be drawn.

The first thing you must decide is whether you will select a sample based on probability or nonprobability sampling methods. This decision is dependent on several factors, including how you plan to use the information you have collected and the constraints you will face in selecting a sample (accessibility of potential participants, time, and expense).

For example, if your ultimate goal is to use data collected from a sample to make statements about a larger group of people (as in some descriptive studies), probability sampling methods will be required. However, this goal will have to be balanced against the difficulty, time, and expense of drawing a probability sample from a well-defined population. If your ultimate goal is less concerned with the generalizability of your findings and more concerned with presenting detailed information about personal experiences (as in some exploratory studies) or evaluating a program or intervention (outcomes evaluation), then you may choose to select a nonprobability sample.

Probability samples are preferred for survey methods. Single-subject and group designs for program evaluation are typically nonprobability because you are using the clients in your program and do not have a population to draw from. Occasionally, you might be able to draw a probability sample from the clients served by the agency, in which case you should complete Part A.

If you are already certain about which type of sample you want to use, then proceed to Part A if you are going to do a probability sample, Part B if nonprobability. If you are uncertain about which type of sample would work best for your study, then begin with Part A on probability samples, and the questions should help you determine if a probability sample is feasible for your study.

NAME: DATE:

RESEARCH QUESTION:

(A) For probability samples

(1) What is the theoretical population for your study?

(2) What will be your actual study population? Specify the criteria you will establish to determine if someone "fits" within your study population? Example: 1) at least 18 years of age, 2) with at least one child, and 3) a first time recipient of services at the agency. Be sure to specify the time frame (e.g., within the month of March).

(3)   Although the results from your sample are generalizable only to
      your study population, you are of course interested in adding to
      an understanding of the theoretical population. For example, since
      we can't study all the people who are homeless, we study some
      obtainable group of them, and what we learn is added to the body
      of knowledge about homeless people. We are thus required to discuss
      how our study population may differ from the theoretical population
      (only shelter users or only homeless people in small towns). This is
      helpful when trying to understand why findings from one study may
      differ from those of another.

      In what ways will your study population differ from the theoretical
      population?

(4)   What will be the sampling frame (the actual list of potential participants) for your study population? Include either the actual size of the study population or provide your best estimate. Indicate any planned safeguards for obtaining confidential information.

You will probably need to explore this with your field instructor. In some instances you might need to know confidential information about people (diagnoses, problem situations) in order to determine their inclusion in the sampling frame—for example, a study of teens identified as alcohol or drug abusers in a child welfare agency that serves all categories of children. Generally in those situations, agency personnel must first obtain client permission before releasing names to you, even though you are in placement at the agency. This is especially true in large agencies that have several divisions.

Sometimes this ethical consideration is disregarded, and it is your responsibility as an ethical researcher to ensure attention to it. To help you consider how important it is to have client consent for release of information, consider how you would feel if someone was giving to others, without your permission or knowledge, that particular information about you or one of your children.

(5)   Consider any possible biases in your sampling frame—for example, omitted names, organization by single-service users versus multiple-service users, organization by length of service, court referral versus self-referral, repeat listings of the same name, listings by family members. List those biases below and how you either will be able to correct for them or will need to include them in a discussion of your sample's limitations.

(6)   What specific type of probability sample will you choose (simple random, systematic)? Include your rationale, and consider stratification prior to systematic sampling as a means of enhancing the representativeness of your sample. For stratification, on what variable(s) (sample member characteristics) would you stratify and why?

(7) Indicate the specific procedure for sample selection.   Indicate who will screen potential sample members and how they will do it.

(8) When you ask people to participate, some will refuse. You should keep a tally of how many refuse so that you can calculate and report a participation rate. Also, it is helpful later, when considering possible biases of your sample, to compare participants with those who refused to participate. What information could you collect about nonparticipants (from observation, screening questions) that would enable you to make comparisons?

(9)   What size will your sample be? Indicate your rationale and discuss the feasibility of your sample size relative to time, expense, means of contact, and level of difficulty in contact, screening, and selection.

(10)   Pay close attention to the inclusion and representation of people of color, frequently underrepresented in research studies. If you intend to make statements about people of color, how have you ensured that people of color will be included in your sample in sufficient numbers to provide meaningful data about them? (Do NOT report results where you pool several racial or ethnic groups into a category labeled "other." This provides no useful information.)

(11) In summary, state clearly to whom you expect to be able to generalize your findings, based on the sampling plan you have devised.

(12) Discuss the strengths and limitations of your sample design.

(B) For nonprobability samples
    (typically used in outcomes evaluation and qualitative studies)

(1)   What is your specific group of interest?

(2)   What are the possible sources that you have considered for obtaining sample members and the pros and cons of each?

(3)   What are the screening and selection criteria for your sample?

Indicate the specific procedure for sample selection.   Indicate who will screen potential sample members and how they will do it.

You will probably need to explore this with your field instructor. In some instances you might need to know confidential information about people (diagnoses, problem situations) in order to determine their potential inclusion in your sample—for example, a study of teens identified as alcohol or drug abusers in a child welfare agency that serves all categories of children. Generally in those situations, agency personnel must first obtain client permission before releasing names to you, even though you are in placement at the agency. This is especially true in large agencies that have several divisions.

Sometimes this ethical consideration is disregarded, and it is your responsibility as an ethical researcher to ensure attention to it. To help you consider how important it is to have client consent for release, consider how you would feel if someone was giving to others that particular information about you or one of your children.

Indicate any planned safeguards for obtaining confidential information.

(4)   What specific type of sample will you draw?

(5)   What size will your sample be? Indicate your rationale and discuss the feasibility of your sample size relative to time, expense, means of contact, and level of difficulty in contact, screening, and selection.

(6)   Pay close attention to the inclusion of people of color, frequently overlooked in research studies. Indicate below how you will ensure that your study will represent people of color. (Do NOT report results where you pool several racial or ethnic groups into a category labeled "other." This provides no useful information.)

(7)   Discuss the strengths and limitations of your sample design. Because experiences vary across cultures, how will you ensure that your study will reflect those differences?

(C) Write the SAMPLE section

This first draft will be approximately two pages and should cover the details of your sampling design. Later, after you have collected your data, you will add how your sampling procedures actually occurred, including participation rate and the demographic characteristics of your sample members.

For probability samples, if possible, you should compare participants to nonparticipants on any information you may have for both groups (age, race, gender, or social class) to provide information about the extent to which participants are similar to or different from nonparticipants.

PROTECTION OF RESEARCH PARTICIPANTS

REMINDER:

Review your text on the protection of research participants and constructing consent forms.

Earlier you discovered the procedures of the university and agency for protecting research participants and obtaining approval of research studies. Review boards typically require information about the proposed data collection procedures, sample selection, and informed consent, as well as copies of data collection instruments, including interview agenda. You have noted this information in earlier sections of the workbook. Complete the following sections, putting the information into the required format.

Research participants must be provided with information about the study and how it might affect them. A parent or guardian can act on behalf of participants who cannot understand or consent for themselves. With few exceptions, parental consent is required for participants who are under age 18.

When using innocuous and anonymous questionnaires in survey research, a consent form may not be required; however, you have an ethical obligation to provide information about the study to the participants. This is usually done in a cover letter accompanying the survey or questionnaire. Check with your university's IRB for clarification.

Social workers have additional obligations relative to the ethical conduct of research. If you become aware that someone is being abused or might harm themselves or another person, you are obligated to report it to the appropriate agency or authority. If you anticipate situations where this might be revealed, you should include in your consent from that you have a legal responsibility to report these incidents and would be obligated to violate the participant's confidentiality relative to that issue.

NAME: DATE:

RESEARCH QUESTION:

REMINDER:
IRB and agency approval must be obtained before collecting data!

(A) Construct a consent form

(1)   Use the guidelines provided by the university IRB for what to include in the consent form. Although we have included samples of consent forms in this section on pages 155-156, be sure to check with your university's IRB. We recommend that you also ask for a sample consent form from the university IRB or your course instructor. Your methods text will also give information about constructing consent forms. You will submit the consent form along with your packet of information to the IRB. Remember, if you are including persons under age 18 and their parent or guardian, you may need two different consent forms, one for each group.

On separate pages, list each point or item you must include in your consent form according to the university IRB and agency requirements.

(2)   On a separate page, prepare a draft of the consent form. Obtain feedback from your course instructor and agency instructor. Revise and finalize the consent form.

COURSE INSTRUCTOR'S SIGN-OFF:

(B)   Outline procedures for obtaining informed consent

Indicate how you plan to inform participants about the study and obtain their consent to participate. Include specific procedures for children or youth under age 18 if applicable.

Please note that young children are usually asked orally for their assent to participate in a study. If young children are participating in your study, indicate how you will obtain assent from them. Include the script you will use for obtaining assent.

(C) Confidentiality safeguards

(1) Describe how you will protect the privacy and confidentiality of the research participants at the time you collect the data.

(2) Describe your plans for storage and protection of data, including the signed consent forms. Also, indicate a date at which point your data will be destroyed. We recommend you include this information in your consent form.

(3) Describe your plans for protecting privacy and confidentiality in your presentation of findings and written report.

(D) Request agency approval

Indicate the steps you have taken for agency approval of your study. (The agency may or may not have a specific process for approval of research. If there is no agency process in place, we encourage you to obtain written permission to carry out the study from the director of the agency.)

(E)   Request IRB approval

(1)   Using what you have written in the workbook, prepare the information requested by the university and agency IRBs.

(2)   Have your course instructor review the information before you submit it to the IRBs. Ask the instructor to initial and date here.

Course Instructor's Sign-off:

Sample Informed Consent Form

We would like you to participate in the Evaluation of *[program name]*. Your participation is important to us and will help us assess the effectiveness of the program. As a participant in *[program name]* we will ask you to *[complete a questionnaire, answer questions in an interview, or other task]*.

We will keep all of your answers confidential. Your name will never be included in any reports and none of your answers will be linked to you in any way. The information that you provide will be combined with information from everyone else participating in the study.

[If information/data collection includes questions relevant to behaviors such as child abuse, drug abuse, or suicidal behaviors, the program should make clear its potential legal obligation to report this information—and that confidentiality may be broken in these cases. Make sure that you know what your legal reporting requirements are before you begin your evaluation.]

You do not have to participate in the evaluation. Even if you agree to participate now, you may stop participating at any time or refuse to answer any question. Refusing to be part of the evaluation will not affect your participation or the services you receive in *[program name]*.

If you have any questions about the study you may call *[name and telephone number of evaluator, program manager, or community advocate]*.

By signing below, you confirm that this form has been explained to you and that you understand it.

Please Check One:

☐   AGREE TO PARTICIPATE

☐   DO NOT AGREE TO PARTICIPATE

_____Signed
Participant or Parent/Guardian

_____Date

From: United State Department of Health and Human Services. (1997). *The Program Manager's Guide to Evaluation, p. 77.*

**Informed Consent to Participate with the University of ____
in the Survey of Persons Who Are Homeless**

I understand that participation in this study involves the following:

1. **Why is the study being conducted?** Dr. ___ of the University of ____ is conducting a study to find out more about people who use shelters, meal programs, and drop-in centers in this county. I have been asked to take part because I have used one of these facilities.

2. **What am I being asked to do?** I will be one of about 500 adults in the county who are interviewed about their childhood experiences, housing and job history, and current feelings about life in general. I will be asked what some people consider to be sensitive questions about alcohol and drug use, mental illness, and criminal conduct. If I am a parent, I will be interviewed about my children. I will be asked questions about my children's physical health, school experiences, mental health, living situation, any problem behaviors, and his or her general outlook on life. The interview usually takes about 90 minutes. I will also be asked to participate in two additional interviews over the course of a year. I will be asked to let the researchers on this project review any records I may have with the County Mental Health Services to monitor my current and past contact to help locate me in the future. I will be interviewed on the premises of this shelter/meal program.

3. **Is this voluntary?** Yes. I am under no obligation to participate. If I agree to participate, I can ask the interviewer to skip any questions that I'd rather not answer. Also, I am free to stop the interview at any time. I am also free to decline to participate in the follow-up surveys or any other aspects of the study.

4. **What are the advantages of participating?** Participating in this study will help the University make recommendations to policy makers that could affect the types of services that are available to help people who find themselves in need. In addition, I will receive $10 for participating in this interview and $25 each for two more interviews over the next year.

5. **Will participating in this study affect the services I am receiving?** No. Whether or not I agree to participate in the study will not affect the type or amount of services I am eligible to receive.

6. **Is this confidential?** Yes. Nothing learned about me by the researchers will be told to anyone else. The study staff will remove identifying information from my completed questionnaire. All records will be identified only by a number, and the link between that number and my name will be kept in a locked file that is available only to the senior investigators. Once the study is completed, all records of my name will be destroyed. All data will be kept in locked files. Everything that I say is strictly confidential, and any reports or other published data based on this study will appear only in the form of summary statistics without the names of or other identifying information about participants. This study has been granted a "Confidentiality Certificate" from the government. For more information about this, please see the attached sheet.

7. **What risks do I face if I participate?** There are no risks expected if I answer the questions.

8. **Who do I contact if I have questions about this research?** If I have any questions about the study, I can ask any of the interviewers here or call Dr. ____ at _____.

AI. My signature below indicates that I consent to be interviewed, that I have been given a copy of this consent form, and that I have read and understood it.

Signature:_____ Date:

A2. Witnessed by:
Signature:_____ Date:

Used by permission.

DATA ANALYSIS

This section of the workbook is divided into five areas: (A) presentation of descriptive information, (B) data analysis for survey studies, (C) data analysis for qualitative studies, (D) data analysis for single-subject studies, and (E) data analysis for group design studies.

First decide whether you will do hand tabulation or computer data entry. The advantages of the latter should be obvious, but access to computers and computer expertise are not universal, and consequently, for some, hand tabulation will be necessary.

The discussion that follows is applicable to both hand and computer calculation, but the technical aspects of computer analysis (data file development and statistical programming) will not be covered. If your agency is large enough to support computer analysis, we recommend that you rely upon the expertise of the appropriate agency staff in setting up your data file and programming.

(A) Presentation of descriptive information

(1) Frequencies

The most basic level of analysis involves calculating how many people gave a certain response to each question in the interview or questionnaire. These are called the frequency distributions. You may choose to group some categories of responses together rather than report each one of a long series of responses. For example, rather than report how many people were of every age between 20 and 69, you can group categories together such as 18-19, 20-29, 30-39, etc., and report the number of participants who fall within each category. Be sure to consult a text for assistance in constructing your intervals.

NAME: DATE:

RESEARCH QUESTION:

For continuous variables you may also report (or report only) the means of variables (and other associated statistics), as discussed in the next section.

On a separate sheet, for each variable in your study, list the frequencies of the responses.

(2)   Means

Reporting averages requires that the variables be continuous (such as age, income, etc.) rather than discrete (gender, race, religion, etc.).

You might be interested in knowing the average (mean) of all the responses to a particular question, e.g., the average age of the participants in your study. In such a case you must either ask the computer programmer to "do a run" for you that will calculate the averages (or means) of selected variables, or you will have to calculate the averages by hand.

Knowing the median (middle) value of the variable is also quite informative. This can be calculated by hand or computer as well. You should consult a text for clarification about which statistic is warranted when.

For each of the continuous variables in your study, calculate and report the mean and median response. List them on a separate page.

If you are using a computer for data analysis, calculate and report also the standard deviations for your continuous variables.

(3)   Decide which frequencies to present in your report and determine the order in which you will present them. Often more than one table is helpful. For example, one table may present the characteristics of the sample and another may present frequencies on the key variables in your study. Begin with general information and move to specific findings, reflecting the focus of your study.

To help organize your presentation of findings, make two lists: primary findings and secondary findings. The primary findings should relate directly to your research question and should be given the most attention in your narrative and visual presentations.

List your primary and secondary findings below, and indicate what will be presented in table form by sketching the tables.

(4)   Determine what findings would best be represented in graphs. Sketch them below.

(5)   We encourage researchers to share findings with the research participants, or when that is not possible (e.g., anonymous participants), with similar people.

Indicate your plan for sharing the study findings with participants.

(B)   Data analysis for survey studies

Once you have tabulated the basic descriptive data in your study for presentation, you should consider if there are other ways to present your data that might shed more light on your findings and answer additional research questions.

Group comparisons, which are really bivariate (two variable) analyses, are most often considered. Often people are interested in knowing how different groups of people compare on certain characteristics. For example, in a needs assessment, you may be interested in knowing if there are differences in identified needs (variable 1) between men and women (variable 2) or in number of sessions attended (variable 1) for self-referred individuals and court-referred individuals (variable 2) in an outcome evaluation. Conducting a group comparison will provide that information.

On the following page, list in columns the groups you would like to compare. In rows to the left of the columns list the variables on which you would like to compare the groups. (See our example below. We compare males and females on four variables.)

You can either give this list to a computer programmer for calculation or do the calculations yourself by arranging the individual data sheets into piles representing the groups you have chosen. For each group, calculate the descriptive statistics—for example, the frequency, mean, percentage, or median—of the responses to each variable in which you are interested. Enter them in the appropriate cells in tables on a separate sheet.

Be sure to include the sample n and group n's, and also the group percentages for comparison purposes. Examine your empirical articles for examples of tables.

Table 1
Variables by Gender

Variables	Male n = 120	Female n = 40
Respondents with school disciplinary actions	10% (12)	8% (3)
Mean age	16.2	17.3
(Standard deviation)	(1.7)	(1.4)
Median age	16	17
Witnessed violent act	30% (36)	25% (10)
Attitudes toward violence scale		
Mean	25	32
(Standard Deviation)	(5.6)	(10.2)
Median	21	22

(C) Data analysis for qualitative studies

Recall that the goal of qualitative research is to provide an in-depth understanding of a phenomenon from the perspective of the research participants. Strategies for qualitative analysis vary and can be quite complicated.

Your aim as a novice researcher is to conduct an analysis that organizes and summarizes the textual accounts of your participants and incorporates your observations. Your task is to identify themes and patterns in the data and offer interpretations of them. First, you will reduce the pages of data, your notes and observations, to a summarization of common topics and themes that participants have presented, with the goal of answering your research question. Next, you will organize the topics and themes, and select some representative quotes to illustrate your main points. Finally, you will offer your interpretation of the findings and your explanation for similarities and differences in, or exceptions to, the findings.

We strongly suggest that you type the data (either in its entirety or at a minimum, the portions of the interviews that address your research topic) into a word processor.

REMINDER:

Review a text specifically devoted to qualitative methods. A general research text may not provide enough information for you to conduct a good qualitative analysis.

---

(1) Read through all the data: the interviews, your notes, and any other sources of data you have. As you read (and you should read through your data several times), identify the common topics that respondents discuss. Keep a list of all the topics you identify.

Read through the data until you cannot identify any new topics. List your topics on separate pages.

(2) Identify excerpts of data (sections of each participant's responses) that relate to the topics you have identified. Excerpts can range from a portion of a sentence to several paragraphs or pages. Place textual excerpts in the topic areas you have identified. Here is where a word processor is invaluable. You can easily block, move, and copy excerpts into topic files.

During this process, you may identify new topics that you had not previously thought of. Add them to your list.

(3) For each topic area, identify themes (categories) across the participants' responses. Ask yourself:

✓ What are the main themes that are important to answering my research question?

✓ What similarities and differences do I see in the responses?

✓ Are there any trends or patterns across responses?

✓ Are there exceptions to the themes I have identified?

(4) Arrange themes to answer research questions. Be sure to include each participant's voice in your presentation.

✓ Which themes seem to belong together?

✓ What order of presentation of themes makes sense to you?

(5) Data display

(a) Select representative excerpts and anecdotal accounts from each main theme. Provide enough excerpts and illustrations so that the reader can "see" how you arrive at the findings. List them on other pages to include in your final paper.

(b) What tables or graphs are appropriate for displaying your data, if any? Sketch them on separate pages.

(6)   If possible obtain feedback from your research participants regarding the themes, trends, and patterns you identified. Write their feedback on separate pages and include their feedback in your final report.

CAUTION:

You are reporting findings based on the people in your study only. You must be careful to avoid using findings to generalize to others. Rather, your study is exploratory and offers tentative suggestions that require further study. For a discussion of trustworthiness, credibility, dependability, and generalization, review a qualitative methods text.

(D) Data analysis for single-subject studies

We encourage researchers to share study findings with the research participants, or when that is not possible (e.g., anonymous participants), with similar people. In single-subject studies, however, the researcher as practitioner and the client share constant feedback during the intervention phase. When the study is completed, the researcher can review the results with the client by using the graphed data, which are the focus of the data analysis outlined below.

The significance of your single-subject study findings can be evaluated in three ways: visual significance, statistical significance, and substantive (clinical) significance.

(1)   Visual significance

   (a)   On a separate sheet draw a graph of your findings with
        the X and Y axes clearly marked as well as all baseline and
        intervention phases. Connect the plotted points on the graph,
        and comment below on the visual significance of your findings.

(b) What changes in the target goal do you observe? What is the trend at baseline and at intervention?

(c) Does it appear that the intervention was effective, ineffective, or unclear? Support your answer.

(2)   Statistical significance

There are several procedures available for determining statistical significance in single-subject studies. Refer to a text, and seek your instructor's assistance as you choose one of the following methods: celeration line, two standard deviation procedure, proportion/frequency procedure.

Complete one test, detailing how it was done and the final results.

(3)   Substantive/clinical significance

Comment on the clinical significance of your findings.

(E) Data analysis for outcomes evaluations using group designs

(1)   For one group pretest-posttest design

In a separate table you should present each of the pretest and posttest measures for your study sample, making sure to include the number in the group at each point. To statistically examine the change for participants from baseline (when pretest measures were taken) to the end of the intervention (when posttest measures are taken), you must conduct a dependent groups t test (also referred to as a correlated groups t test, a paired groups t test, and matched groups t test). This allows you to determine whether the change (if there *was* a change) in the outcome measure from pre to post is large enough that it would indicate change that was more than just random fluctuation in the data.

If your data have been entered into a data analysis program, do this statistical test and include the results in the table. If you are doing calculations by hand, consult a statistics text for the dependent groups t-test formula, and calculate the statistic, including the statistic in the table.

Fill in the table below to present the outcome results. Include a statistical test of the change. Consider other examples in your empirical articles.

Table 1
Table name

Time	Measure 1 n =	Measure 2 n =
Pretest		
Posttest		

t =   , df =   , p =   .

(2)   For control and comparison group designs

In a separate table you should present each of the pretest and posttest measures for your study sample, making sure to include the number in the group at each point.

To statistically examine the change for participants from baseline (when pretest measures were taken) to the end of the intervention (when posttest measures are taken), you must first consider whether your outcomes are discrete or continuous measures. For measures that are discrete you will perform a cross-tabulation and report a chi-square statistic. For measures that are continuous you will conduct an independent groups t-test. Both tests allow you to determine whether the difference (if there *was* a difference) in the outcome measure between your treatment group and your comparison (or control) group is large enough that it indicates a difference between groups that is more than just random fluctuation in the data.

If your data have been entered into a data analysis program, do this statistical test and include the results in the table. If you are doing calculations by hand, consult a statistics text for the formulas, and calculate the statistics, including the results in the table.

(a)   For discrete variables

Sketch below your table presenting the outcome results.
Include a chi-square statistical test of the differences between
the two groups. Look for examples in your empirical articles.

Table 1
Table name

Group	Pretest n =	Posttest n =
Treatment Group		
Control Group		

$x^2=$, df =   , p =   .

(b)   With a continuous dependent variable

Sketch below your table presenting the outcome results.
Include an independent groups t-test.   Look for examples in
your empirical articles.

Table 1
Table name

Time	Treatment Group	Control Group
Pretest		
	(n =)	(n =)
Posttest		
	(n =)	(n =)
t = , df = , p = .		

WRITING THE FINAL PAPER

Allow enough time to write your research report! Having completed each section of the workbook, you have a rough draft of your paper, but the final paper should not be written hastily. We recommend that you follow the outline at the end of this section, and write a revised draft to share with your field instructor, agency staff, and peers for feedback and comments. You may also seek help from your school's writing center.

This section focuses on presenting your findings in a written research paper. Basically, your report will include what you did and why, what you found, and what it means. From this paper, you can develop a presentation for your agency, for your peers in field placement, or for participants at a conference. If you are interested in submitting your study for publication, check with your course instructor for guidance.

Remember, you have already written a first draft of the paper, so you have a good start! Your research paper will expand on earlier sections and include new sections on findings and discussion. Refer to the Research Paper Outline at the end of this section.

(A)   Rewrite earlier sections of your paper

Revise earlier drafts of the Introduction, Literature Review, and Methods sections, changing the tense from future (you will study) to past (you studied). Incorporate the feedback you received from your course instructor, field instructor, and others along the way.

In the methods section, be sure to discuss your procedures for obtaining informed consent and how you protected the confidentiality of your research participants.

(B) For the *Sample* section

Revise your draft of **Section X** and include the results of your sampling procedures.

(1)   Describe the criteria and procedures for sample selection as they were carried out in your study.

(2)   Present the results of the sampling procedures, the response rate, and demographic characteristics of the sample members.

(3)   If you conducted survey research, compare the participants to those who refused to participate.

(C) Write the *Findings* section

Drawing from **Section XII** of the workbook, on separate pages organize and present the findings of your study.

(1)   In narrative form, present your primary and secondary findings.

(2)   Visually and textually display data that will help the reader understand your findings.

    (a)   When appropriate, display data in tables, graphs, or charts.

    (b)   Sketch out the tables, graphs, or charts you plan to use. You may want to get help to do the final graphics on a computer.

    (c)   Write the narrative section for the body of the paper and describe visual displays.

(3)   For qualitative studies, you will use excerpts identified in **Section XII** to illustrate themes.

(4)   Review the findings section of your report to be sure that you present the *results* of your study, not your interpretation of them.

(D)   Write the *Discussion* section

Refer to the Research Paper Outline for the topics to be included. Use the following questions to list the main points to be included in this section. After you have answered each question, write the full draft of the discussion section.

(1)   Discuss your interpretation of the findings

(a)   Refer to your original research question and discuss what you learned about it.

(b)   Refer to the literature you reviewed and comment on how your findings relate to that literature.

(2)   Develop implications for social work

What do the findings of your study mean for the agency, staff members, the participants, and/or the social work profession?

(3)   Provide recommendations for social workers

Based on your study, what policies, programs, and/or practice actions do you think should be taken by your agency or social work practitioners?

(4)   Report the limitations of your study relative to measures, data collection procedures, and sample design.

(5)   Make suggestions for future research

What would you recommend to the next researcher who wants to study this topic? List questions that emerged from your study that you think future research should address.

(E) Compile the *References*

Include all the sources of information (journal articles, books, and reports) that you used in writing your report. Consult a style manual for proper form.

(F) Compile the *Appendices*

Include a copy of the consent form and your research instrument or interview agenda.

(G) Write the *Abstract*

An abstract is a brief overview summary of your study and results, usually 100 words or less. Write the abstract and place it immediately following your title page.

(H) Final checklist

☐ Have you preserved the confidentiality of the research participants?

☐ Have you used gender-neutral language in your report?

☐ Have you properly cited work by other authors that you use in your report?

☐ Have you proofread your paper for grammar, punctuation, and spelling errors?

RESEARCH PAPER OUTLINE

Title Page

Abstract

Introduction
    Significance and purpose of study
    Relevance to social work
    Research question

Literature review
    Theories and concepts and variables
    Empirical studies

Methods
    Research design
    Data collection procedures
    Protections for research participants
    Measures
    Research instrument or interview agenda

Sample
    Procedures
    Characteristics of sample members

Findings
    Visual presentation: Tables, graphs, and charts
    Narrative presentation

Discussion
    Your interpretation of findings
    Implications and recommendations for social work
    Strengths and limitations of the study
    Suggestions for future research

References

Appendices
    Consent form
    Research instrument

BIBLIOGRAPHY

American Psychological Association. (1994). *Publication Manual of the American Psychological Association* (4th ed.). Washington, DC.

Bloom, M., Fischer, J., and Orme, J. G. (1999). *Evaluating Practice: Guidelines for the Accountable Professional* (3rd ed.). Needham Heights, MA: Allyn & Bacon.

Cooper, M. (1990). Treatment of a client with obsessive-compulsive disorder. *Social Work Research and Abstracts* (June), 26-31.

Collins, P., Kayser, K., and Tourse, R. C. (1994). Bridging the gaps: An interdependent model for educating accountable practitioners. *Journal of Social Work Education, 30*(2), 241-251.

Fischer, J., and Corcoran, K. J. (1994). *Measures for clinical practice: Vol. 1. Couples, Families, Children* (2nd ed.). New York: Free Press.

Fischer, J., and Corcoran, K. J. (1994). *Measures for clinical practice: Vol. 2. Adults* (2nd ed.). New York: Free Press.

Epstein, I. (1987). Pedagogy of the perturbed: Teaching research to the reluctants. *Journal of Teaching in Social Work, 1*(1), 71-89.

Fineran, S., and Bennett, L. (1998). Teenage peer sexual harassment: Implications for social work practice in education. *Social Work 43*(1), 55-64.

Forte, J. A., and Mathews, C. (1994). Potential employers' views of the ideal undergraduate social work curriculum. *Journal of Social Work Education, 30*(2), 228-240.

Fraser, M., Lewis, R., and Norman, J. (1991). Research education in MSW programs: An exploratory analysis. *Journal of Teaching in Social Work, 4*(2), 83-103.

Gabor, P. A., Unrau, Y. A., and Grinnell, R. M. (1998). *Evaluation and Quality Improvement in the Human Services* (2nd ed.). Needham Heights, MA: Allyn & Bacon.

Grinnell, R. M. (1997). *Social Work Research and Evaluation* (5th ed.). Itasca, IL: F. E. Peacock.

Jordan, C., and Franklin, C. (1995). *Clinical Assessment for Social Workers: Quantitative and Qualitative Methods*. Chicago: Lyceum Books.

Kirk, S. A. (1990). Research utilization: The substruction of belief. In L. Videka-Sherman and W. J. Reid (Eds.), *Advances in Clinical Social Work Research*. Silver Spring, MD: National Association of Social Workers Press.

Kirk, S., and Fischer, J. (1976). Do social workers understand research? *Journal of Education for Social Work, 12*, 63-70.

Knight, C. (1993). A comparison of advanced standing and regular master's students' performance in the second-year field practicum: Field instructors' assessments. *Journal of Social Work Education, 29*(3), 309-317.

Kurtz, P. D., Jarvis, S. V., and Kurtz, G. L. (1991). Problems of homeless youths: Empirical findings and human service issues. *Social Work, 36*(4), 309-314.

Leedy, P. D. (1996). *Practical Research: Planning and Design.* New York: Prentice Hall.

Lincoln, Y. S., and Guba, E. G. (1985). *Naturalistic Inquiry.* Beverly Hills, CA: Sage.

Marino, R., Green, R., and Young, E. (1998). Beyond the scientist-practitioner model's failure to thrive: Social workers' participation in agency-based research activities. *Social Work Research, 22*(3), 188-192.

Marlow, C. (1997). *Research Methods for Generalist Social Work Practice* (2nd ed.). Pacific Grove, CA: Wadsworth.

Patton, M. Q. (1990). *Qualitative Evaluation Methods.* Newbury Park, CA: Sage.

Report of the NIMH Task Force on Social Work Research. (1991, November).

Riessman, C. K. (1997). *Qualitative Studies in Social Work Research.* Newbury Park, CA: Sage.

Roberts, C., Piper, L., Denny, J., and Cuddeback, G. (1997). A support group intervention to facilitate young adults' adjustment to cancer. *Health and Social Work, 22,* 133-141.

Royse, D. (1999). *Research Methods in Social Work* (3rd ed.). Chicago, IL: Nelson-Hall.

Rubin, A., and Babbie, E. (1997). *Research Methods for Social Work* (3rd ed.). Pacific Grove, CA: Wadsworth.

Siegel, D. H. (1993). Open adoption of infants: Adoptive parents' perceptions of advantages and disadvantages. *Social Work, 38*(1), 15-23.

Strom, K., and Gingerich, W. (1993). Educating students for the new market realities. *Journal of Social Work Education, 29*(1), 78-87.

Williams, M., Tutty, L. M., and Grinnell, R. M. (1995). *Research in Social Work: An Introduction* (2nd ed.). Itasca, IL: F. E. Peacock.

Yegidis, B. L., Weinbach, R. W., and Morrison-Rodgriguez, B. (1998). *Research Methods for Social Workers* (3rd ed.). Englewood Cliffs, NJ: Prentice Hall.

York, R. O. (1997). *Conducting Social Work Research: An Experiential Approach.* Needham Heights, MA: Allyn & Bacon.